The
Ghost Hunter's
BIBLE

The Definitive Edition
Published 2002
www.zerotime.com

6-18-2004

Trent Brandon

The Ghost Hunter's Bible
The Definitive Edition

Copyright 2000-2004 by Trent Brandon & Zerotime Publishing.

Written by: Trent Brandon
trent@zerotime.com

Cover Art and Artwork: Chris Pugh
Book Design: Chris Pugh
Editor: Lisa Rupple
Editor: Tiffiny Kirsch
Publisher Assistant: Tiffiny Kirsch

This book is subject to revisions when deemed applicable to keep it current with technical advances in the ghost hunting field and new scientific research.

Published by,
Zerotime Publishing in Association with Zerotime Paranormal
http://www.zerotime.com/

Zerotime Publishing books are available at special discounts when purchased in bulk quantities for businesses, associations, institutions or sales promotions. Please contact trent@zerotime.com or visit our website at http://www.zerotime.com/

ISBN: 0-9703100-5-6
Printed in the United States of America
All Rights Reserved

Version 1.5

The Ghost Hunter's Bible
Table of Contents

This book is dedicated to all of the ghost hunters who search for truth.

A huge "thank you" goes out to the following:

The Zerotime Paranormal Team:
Chris Alexander, Tiffiny Cope, Frank Ippolito, Chris Pugh, Lisa Rupple and Chad Weese.
Tiffiny Cope who spent all of her vacation time developing the book.
Monica Reed and the members of The Mansfield Reformatory Preservation Society (MRPS).
Cathy Prudy and BookMasters, Inc. Mansfield Ohio - Great Book Printers!
Emil DeToffol at Less EMF Inc. Emil runs a super business!
The Geauga County Sheriff's Deputies.
Gary Lawrence, a good freelance writer and a professional ghost hunter.
Jan and George Newton, The Baltimore Street Bed and Breakfast, Gettysburg PA.
Dave Oester & Sharon Gill, founders of the International Ghost Hunters Society.
Dunkin Donuts, and the local Chili's Restaurant - The chicken crispers rule!
The Jerkey Hut. The world's best beef jerky! A must have food for all ghost hunts!
The employees of Six Flags Amusement Park, Worlds of Adventure & Fright Fest.
CoreComm Web Site Hosting - Finally, a good company to host my website!
Workers at the local Minerva Post Office. I know they get tired of shipping my packages.
Ashtabula Digital, created a great computer system at a very cheap price.
Publishers Marketing Association (PMA) - Publishing Assistance.
All of the hard working ghost hunters out there who email me encouraging letters.
Tasha Nutter - My good friend even though she is terrified of ghosts.

The New York City Police Officers and Fire Fighters.
In Memory of 9-11-2001

The Ghost Hunter

The paranormal is a world steeped in mystery. The Ghost Hunter's Bible was created with the needs of the ghost hunter in mind. This book will take you through the *Methods of Conducting a Ghost Hunt*, from explaining what types of technical equipment you should have and how to use them, to how to conduct an investigation and interview witnesses. After you cover the basics you can move on to *What Ghost Hunters Should Know*, a chapter designed to enhance your overall paranormal knowledge. The *Parapsychology* chapter touches on the intense science involved in paranormal investigation, and the relationships between the paranormal and the world we live in. The comprehensive entity lists in the chapter, *Things that Go Bump* provide future ghost hunters with easy reference access to many of the most common paranormal anomalies. *Famous Ghost Stories* provides examples of ghosts and haunts and what to expect when studying the paranormal. This book provides guidance for amateur and professional ghost hunters.

Questions commonly asked:

Who qualifies to call himself or herself a ghost hunter?
What does a person have to do to become a ghost hunter?

Those two questions are easy to answer. Anyone can qualify to be called a ghost hunter. The job spectrum ranges from the professional who travels the world with high tech equipment to the weekend ghost hunter tape-recording strange noises in the attic. Anyone curious enough to explore the supernatural unknown is a ghost hunter. Academic degrees and awards are fantastic, but they alone will not make someone a "good" ghost hunter. Ghost hunting is a profession. It's a technical craft where most of the knowledge will be self-taught and learned directly on the job by working along side other ghost hunters as an apprentice. To be successful as a ghost hunter you will need to study and understand the theories and methods of ghost hunting and learn how to apply them in the field. You will need to understand what type of ghost you might be dealing with and how its characteristics will affect your investigation. You will need to practice using the tools of the trade, and most importantly, you will have to develop a keen intuition. Most ghost hunters already believe in ghosts. The drive to understand the very nature and origins of the human soul draw people into this field. The toughest part of becoming a responsible ghost hunter is learning how to go into each ghost hunt with the mind of a skeptic. It is the ghost hunter's duty to be open-minded and examine the facts of every case for any logical explanations or possible frauds. The word open-minded does not mean solely believing in the existence of ghosts and not accepting any other theories. Ghost hunters must be fair, rational, and always searching for logical explanations. It is the job of the paranormal investigator to uncover the absolute truth, no matter what that truth may be. There are thousands of ghost hunters, but only a handful of good paranormal investigators. Reading this book will make you a better and more knowledgeable paranormal investigator.

What are ghosts?

Ghosts present science with its greatest puzzle by eluding the reality of the physical world. They play tricks on the human senses; confusing the mind with unexplained noises in the middle of the night, locking doors from the inside of empty rooms, and fading apparitions that toy with the realm of existence. Science has no current method to examine or experiment with the supernatural. History has shown time-and-time again that when mainstream science encounters the unexplainable it is immediately written off as nonsense. What is happening? Credible witnesses see ghosts everyday. Smart, well-educated people have reported strange encounters with the supernatural. After staying over in the Lincoln Bedroom at the White House, Queen Wilhelmina of the Netherlands said that she was awakened by a strange knock on her bedroom door in the middle of the night. She got up from her bed and answered the door only to be confronted with the ghost of President Abraham Lincoln, who vanished into thin air seconds later. Past American presidents, Theodore Roosevelt, Herbert Hoover and Harry Truman all reported hearing unexplained rapping noises on their bedroom doors at night, and many of them felt as if they were being watched while standing in the Lincoln bedroom. They all believed that the ghost of Lincoln was haunting the White House. Ghost stories have been told and retold since the dawn of history. The Epic Of Gilgamesh traces the belief and experiences with ghosts back to 2000 B.C. Whether mainstream science wants to admit it or not, something is happening.

Rational ghost hunters have studied and investigated supernatural phenomenon for decades, they have provided some clear-cut theories that mainstream science was unwilling or unable to do. Despite the intense scrutiny of science and its claims that a supernatural world does not exist, many of the theories made by early ghost hunters still stand today. However, much is still unknown about ghosts, and so the work must continue.

Do reasonable people believe in ghosts?

Over 80% of people polled believe in the existence of ghosts. Mainstream science and hardcore critics tend to make up the remaining minority percentage, discouraging the rest of the public about coming forward with ghost sightings. As ghost hunters always find, there is no shortage of people with ghost stories to tell. Some people may have never told their story before out of fear that their friends and peers would ridicule them. It is important for those people who have seen ghosts or had a supernatural experience to know that they are not alone. When people begin to share stories, they will find out very quickly that others have had the same types of experiences. We are not alone!

What makes up a "good" ghost hunter?

Ghost hunters should enter a hunt as a detective would; taking notes, doing interviews, researching locations and background, taking pictures and video, and finally, conducting a stakeout or in our case a ghost hunt. The detective side of a ghost hunter has to be aware of all logical and natural explanations and do their best to find a reasonable conclusion. The forensics aspect of ghost hunting is the skill that most ghost hunters fail to develop. A ghost hunter should treat each alleged haunted location like a crime scene. They must meticulously go over the area and carefully gather any physical evidence while not disturbing the environment of the scene. Drawing maps and diagrams of the layout, staging reenactments, and analyzing the smallest of clues that may have been left behind are essential. The final side of a good ghost hunter is the role of public debater. Once all the information and evidence has been gathered, the time comes to defend your conclusions. Like a well-educated attorney, you must have a vast working knowledge of not only your particular case, but also any other similar cases that might help. A ghost hunter must be knowledgeable in their field to remain credible. Critics and scientists are not easy opponents, and if there are flaws in the investigation or the final conclusions, they will point them out in a non-constructive manner.

When hunting for ghosts, do not look for any rules or absolutes. There are circumstances that seem to create a more ghostly atmosphere, but there are no guarantees for predicting when and where a ghost will appear. A ghost may appear once in a hundred years or once every Tuesday. Ghosts can haunt houses or dwell in a small spot in an open field. Even when conditions are perfect for a ghost it does not mean that one will ever show up. In fact, even the appearance of a ghost does not follow any special pattern. In some cases, their presence is nothing more than a sharp chill, in other cases the ghosts cannot be distinguished from a living person. Visitors to Alcatraz in San Francisco Bay are often greeted with a powerful cold gust of air that seems to float around inside the cellblocks and follow people through the prison. This sharp chill is believed to be the ghost of inmates who suffered while imprisoned in "the Rock." Although the ghosts are rarely seen, they can be felt.

A Surgeon driving to work at a Denver hospital tells of a strange encounter with a ghost. He pulled over when he saw a blood-soaked woman standing by the edge of the road waving her arms frantically. She was standing close to an old car that was smashed around a thick tree. The doctor got out to help the women, who explained that her two children where still trapped inside the car. The doctor opened his passenger side door and told the lady to sit down before she passed out. She thanked him for this kindness as the doctor went to retrieve a blanket from the trunk of the car. The doctor said that he only took his eyes off the scene for a few moments, but when he looked up the car and the woman were gone. His exact words describing the incident were, "The woman didn't look like a ghost. She looked solid until the moment she vanished." The doctor discovered later that a woman and her two children were killed in that location many years before when a drunk driver ran them off of the road. The Alcatraz story and the doctor's tale show us the diversity that ghost hunters can expect to experience when investigating the paranormal.

Ghosts can also be in the forms of animals, headless bodies or even something as simple as a ghostly hand carrying a book through a dark hallway. A phantom bear haunts the Tower of London. The sightings began back in the winter of 1815 when sentries on patrol spotted a bear on the grounds at exactly midnight. The guard lunged at the bear with his bayonet, but his weapon passed straight through it. The guard was so terrified that he passed out. It was later discovered that it was common to see spectral animals roaming the grounds. King Henry I kept large zoo animals such as lions, tigers, monkeys, exotic birds and bears at the tower until a lion mauled a soldier. The bear, lion and mauled soldier all continue to haunt the Tower of London.

According to Scotland's MacKenzie, clan the ghost of a spectral hand carrying a silver candlestick haunts them. The sighting of the disembodied hand means that a grim event, usually a death, is soon to follow. This ghost has been seen by members of the MacKenzie family for hundreds of years and continues to be seen to the present time. The hand only appears for a few seconds before vanishing slowly. It is described as a slender hand having tapering fingers and almond-shaped nails, clearly belonging to a woman. The forms that ghosts can take shock and amaze even the most seasoned ghost hunters. Ghosts have been known to interact with the living or just make acknowledgment with a quick glance or eye contact. In other accounts, the ghosts seem unaware of the presence of living people and appear to be acting out some part of their own past life.

When it comes to ghost hunting the only rule is, *be ready for anything!*

Methods of a Ghost Hunt

Tools of the Trade

The list of valuable ghost hunting equipment is constantly growing. This section is divided into three categories: Basic Necessary Equipment, Spirit Detection Devices, and Optional Equipment. High tech gadgets can be very helpful in aiding a good ghost hunter who knows the proper use of each piece of equipment. It is vital to understand the function and use of each high tech gadget. Always experiment with each piece of ghost hunting equipment for several days or weeks before attempting to use them in the field. Give yourself time to learn and practice all of the different, and sometimes complicated, functions. A delicate balance exists when it comes to the use of equipment in ghost hunts. Do not become solely dependent upon equipment. Know your own limitations and bring along only the essential items. All of the equipment in the world will not help if you neglect to develop a keen intuition in the ghost-hunting field.

Basic Necessary Equipment:

Always have the items in this section ready for use in any investigation. These items are cheap, easy to obtain, and can fill a small case.

- Business Cards: Include your name and contact information.
- Notebook and Pens/Pencils: Notebooks are used to keep case notes, log records of events, and personal journal information.
- Flashlights/Candles: Have at least two flashlights with extra batteries. Candles can be used, but are unreliable for staying lit.
- Tape Recorder and Blank Tapes: use a quality full size tape recorder and a separate external static free microphone. Always use brand new blank tapes, never record over old tapes.

- Tape Measure: 12 to 50 feet.
- White Ball of String: 100 feet.
- Scissors and/or Knife.
- Wristwatch.
- Drawing Paper: Plain white drawing or sketch paper.
- Thermometer: A thermometer can detect changes in room temperature. It is good to carry an old-fashioned mercury thermometer. There are electronic (digital) thermometers on the market that are good, but in some cases they have been reported to fail where electromagnetic forces are present.
- Compass: Great for navigation and also can be used for picking up electromagnetic forces. A compass will react to any magnetic or electrical stimuli that are reported in haunting cases.
- Chalk: Use white or colored chalk to mark areas.
- Area Maps: If possible.
- Cotton balls for putting by window and doorways to determine movement.
- Label gun and labels.
- Twist ties or small bendable clamps to keep items bound together.
- Talcum powder: To put on the floors to detect movement.
- Liquid Level Ruler: Used to determine slanted areas.
- Holy cross, Bible, and any other religious symbols.
- First Aid Kit: Always have a first aid kit ready.
- Personal ID and some Spare Cash: Never leave home without them.

Ghost Detection Devices:

In the hands of a prepared ghost hunter these items can be extremely helpful.

- EMF (Electro-Magnetic Field) Detectors: These devices can pick up electronic and magnetic fields over different frequencies. When ghosts are present, they disrupt the electromagnetic fields. EMF detectors will detect these disruptions. These devices can be found relatively cheap, ranging from $25 to $200. As a guideline each person in your ghost-hunting group should have one EMF detector on hand.

- Infrared Thermal Scanner: Infrared scanners save time by accurately pin pointing abnormal cold or hot spots in the area. This is a device that must be tested before using in the field. Expect to spend anywhere from $99 to $500 on this device, depending on the instrument's functions and degree of accuracy. This is not something that you must have, but if you can afford it, give it a try.

• Audio Recorders: Cassette recorders and digital audio recorders can be an important piece of equipment. Ghost hunters find that strange noises or ghostly voices can be recorded at haunted locations, which were inaudible at the time to human ears. Good audio recorders can provide valuable paranormal evidence that you would not get from any other piece of equipment. Audio recorders can run anywhere from $25 to $100 depending upon the features and size.

• Air Ion Counter: These devices measure positive and negative ions in the surrounding air. This little add-on is a good instrument to have, but the price is high at $400 to $600.

• Ghost Catcher (also called a Spirit Wind Chime): This device can be a simple light weight wind chime that you buy in a store or something that you design and create your self. It can be made with parts available in hardware stores. It is very easy and cheap to build, but also a valuable device. A ghost activates the chime as it passes by the ghost catcher and causes it to chime exactly like a wind chime. You can buy the same wind chimes that you find in stores. Try to get chimes made of the lightest metal material so that they are more sensitive. For obvious reasons these will not be effective outside or in any area where a breeze is blowing. Most small wind chimes can be purchased for a few dollars at craft stores.

Optional Equipment:

Items in this section are valuable tools for any investigator. Not everyone can afford to purchase all of these items and that's fine. Keep in mind that ghost hunters made groundbreaking discoveries in the paranormal fields long before most of these items were invented.

• 35 mm Camera: For best results use black and white film or infrared film. Most ghost hunters carry two cameras; one loaded with each. Always buy good quality film and carry a camera light meter to make sure that the pictures turn out with the best quality.

• Instant Camera: For quick photo results these cameras work well. However, most pictures taken with an instant camera that show something strange will be considered either flash errors or hoaxes. Without negatives, there is no way to prove otherwise. These instant cameras are a cheap pickup at $30 plus film.

• Video Camcorders: Most households now own a personal video camera of some kind. The video camera has become an extremely valuable tool for any ghost hunter. It not only gives visual proof of ghost activity, but also helps document investigation sites. Always use brand new, good quality tapes. DON'T FORGET TRIPODS!

• Night Vision Equipment: Night vision equipment is also a new tool to the ghost hunter. Most people think it costs too much, but they are becoming more affordable all the time. A few years ago a night vision scope was unavailable for less than $1,000. Now, you can get very good scopes for $250. There are also adapters (under $30) that will attach the night vision scope directly to a video camcorder. There are even some video cameras that have night vision functions.

• Headset Communicators: When you have a team of three or more people, headset communicators are a great idea for staying in contact when spread out. You could use the handheld walkie-talkies, but the headsets free up your hands for holding cameras or EMF detectors. There are good headsets that work up to distances of 100 yards for $30 each.

• Spot Lights: Small battery powered spot lights really help at night when it comes to setting up and taking down cameras and other equipment. They can be used for safety purposes and to get a better view of the surrounding terrain. Get the lights that sit on the ground and have swivels to set them in different angles. If you have a team of ghost hunters, get between 2 and 6 of these. You can find different versions of these lights at most hardware stores.

• Binoculars: Regular binoculars come in handy from time to time.

• Geiger Counter: This is a very technical and expensive piece of equipment that requires special training to operate correctly. It reads the amount of radiation on the ground, in the air, or on an object. There are certain levels of radiation around us all the time. You will be looking for anything abnormal with this device. The price will vary depending upon the range reading abilities and accuracy of the model. Expect to pay $100 to $1,000. Used models can sometimes be purchased for less than $50 at army surplus stores.

Questionable Equipment:

Two equipment options that ghost hunters sometimes use are Dowsing Rods and Ouija boards. If you are doing a serious scientific investigation do not use either of these methods. The validity of both methods is subject to question. Science does not recognize either of these highly controversial methods. Even under the best working circumstances, Dowsing Rods and Ouija boards have failed to produce consistent working ability. The bottom line is simple - these are not legitimate tools. If you use either, the findings of your investigation will not be taken seriously. Your time and work will be wasted.

Interviewing Witnesses

The most important aspects of an investigation are witness interviews. In most paranormal cases, the testimony of the eyewitness will decide which direction you may take the ghost hunt. If the interview is handled correctly, the information gathered can be very helpful in the rest of the investigation. You must prepare for each interview before conducting it. The same rules apply whether interviewing a total stranger or a member of your own family.

Before the interview begins there are some initial rules of ethics that must be followed:

- Never allow yourself to make a value judgment of the eyewitness based solely on race, education, economic standing, age, sex or any other external appearance.
- Go into every interview believing that the witness is telling the truth.
- Be open-minded and considerate of the feelings of the witness.
- Make conclusions only on the validity of the story after evaluating the evidence gathered from the completed investigation.
- Be prepared to keep the interview on track and explore every possibility, natural and supernatural.
- Always conduct yourself in a professional manner.

Your first key role in the interview is to make the witness feel comfortable. The better the witness feels about the interview the more likely they will be to cooperate without story exaggeration.

Do not conduct interviews with a tired witness. Wait until there is a better time and the witness is fully rested or the information you receive may be incomplete.

Preparing for the Interview:

First, get the number of witnesses. If there is more than one witness always do separate interviews. Each person sees things from their own perspective and this is exactly what you want, the uncontaminated observation of each witness. In a group interview, there is always the risk that one person's testimony will influence the next. Witnesses may feel pressured into saying that they experienced something that they did not simply because the person before them said they did.

The only time that you should have a group of witnesses together is when you return to the scene. Keep in mind that returning to the scene is not always a possibility. Sometimes the witness will refuse or other circumstances prevent it. Returning to the scene usually helps witnesses relive their experience more vividly. It will also provide you with a better visual picture of the details and events that occurred.

Do not pressure the witness to do the interview or to return to the scene. You will run into individuals that seem willing to cooperate, then disappear or back out at the last second. Some may even change their minds in the middle of the interview, which is why it is important to make the witness feel comfortable. If they feel at ease, they will be more likely to finish the full interview. However, if they want to stop the interview and discontinue their arrangement with you for any reason, then that is the end. The interview is over.

Always tell the witness that their names, addresses and other personal information will remain private and stick to that statement. Never give out personal information to anyone, for any reason, without full permission of the witness. All interviews should be videotaped or tape-recorded unless the witness objects. The recording allows you to analyze the interview rather than trying to write everything down. Let the witness know that recorded interviews are only to ensure that the case files are accurate and that only the investigators directly involved will have access to it. Even if you tape the interview take notes. Use them as points of discussion to follow up on. The idea of the interview is to get as much useful information as possible. Some witnesses will object to the videotaped interview, but try to get them because videos are much better than just audio recordings. Video allows you to examine the facial expressions and body language of the witness, which can be very revealing.

Conduct the interview in a relaxed, confusion free atmosphere. Sit comfortably in a well-lit room at a table with only your video camera, tape recorder, pen, and notepad. Make sure that any televisions or stereo systems are turned off. Remove any other distractions and try to avoid interruptions. Have the witness sit directly across from you. When the time feels right, begin the interview.

The Interview:

The interview must begin with the witness retelling their story from start to finish without interruption. All questions should be held off until the witness has finished recounting their full story. During this initial retelling it is the job of the interviewer to listen and take notes. Write down any questions that you want to ask after the witness has finished talking. The wording of your follow-up questions is extremely important. Do not lead the witness! Most interviewers will lead a witness without even knowing that they are doing it, and that is a real fundamental problem. Questions in multiple-choice form or questions asking the witness to speculate are incorrect and useless.

Here are some examples of questions that could occur in a typical interview. Each question has two forms - a leading question and an open-ended question.

Leading: Did you see an apparition, full body ghost or a gray mist?
Open: What did you see?

Leading: Were you frightened?
Open: How did you feel?

Leading: Was the sound a banging or scratching?
Open: What kind of ordinary sound did it remind you of?

You can see the difference in the questions. The leading questions make the witness feel that the only correct answers are the ones offered in the question itself. The open questions leave the witness free to give their exact observations without the pressure that they may give some kind of incorrect answer. Write out twenty or more typical questions and review them. Change them so that they are open-ended questions. Make sure to practice. Like anything else, good interviewing takes practice. Try your best not to ask a leading question, as this could corrupt the entire interview.

Questions that should be asked after the witness's retelling:

- Where were you?
- What were you doing at the time?
- What first caught your attention?
- What did you think it was at first?
- Describe the figure and/or any sounds, odors?
- During the account what were your actions or reactions?
- How did you feel?
- How did the account end?
- What were your reactions directly after this account ended?

Questions Involving Witness Sensory Perceptions:

A huge part of information from a witness will be based on what they SAW, HEARD, FELT and SMELLED. Your duty as the interviewer is to reasonably question the witness on the working ability of their sense of perceptions.

Sense of Sight:

- Does the witness need eye glasses or contact lenses?
- If yes, were they worn at the time of the observation?
- What type of prescription? (Nearsighted/Farsighted/Bifocals/Trifocals)
- Is the witness colorblind?
- Are there any other physical eye problems?

Sense of Hearing:

Witnesses reporting hearing strange sounds must be questioned about any hearing impairment or aids.

- Did the witness have any known hearing impairments?
- Does the witness use a hearing aid?
- If Yes, what kind of hearing aid? Was it worn at the time?
- Were they "actively" listening at the time?

It is also important to keep in mind that there are numerous natural sources that create sound and strange noises. Wind speed and direction can cause sound vibrations. Rustling trees, banging shutters, broken pipes, animals scurrying, buzzing electric lines and mechanical devices are all possible sources for sound misinterpretations.

Sense of Smell:

Strange odors are common in supernatural cases. Every odor needs to be identified and cataloged along with the exact time and location.

- Does the witness have a good sense of smell?
- Can they identify the odor(s) to the best of their abilities?

Sense of Touch:

Falling into this category are sensations of tingling, numbness, levitation, and paralysis. Also included are unseen barriers as well as physical attacks.

- Did the apparition make any physical contact with any witness?
- If Yes, what kind of contact?
- Could the sensation felt been natural? (Hair standing up, Goosebumps, etc.)

Final Notes on Interviewing

After the interviews are complete, find out if any witness has photos or video evidence of the account. If they do, ask to get copies. If no visual proof is available, give them a piece of drawing paper and ask them to draw and label exactly what they experienced. Let the witness know that they don't have to be artists, just have them do their best. Attach all the information gathered from the witness interviews into the final report labeled as evidence.

Do not confuse the witness with a bunch of "jargon" that they would not understand. If you intimidate the witness you will not get the best account. The witness may feel that they need to exaggerate.

Do not try to answer questions that you have no way of knowing, regardless of your conclusions.

Unanswerable Questions:

- Will this happen again?
- Will it come back?
- Am I safe?
- Why did this happen to me?
- What does this mean?

No matter how confident you feel with your answers, the right thing to do is politely decline to answer and explain to the witness that your answers would only be speculation.

If you are able, try to interview the witnesses two or three different times. Conduct an interview at least once at the beginning and once again at the end of the investigation. Look for any inconsistencies that may pop up in the story. If there are inconsistencies, it does not mean that the witness is lying, but they are important to note. Plus, you should take note if anything else has happened to them during the course of your investigation.

In the paranormal investigation field you will run into people who lie, want attention, publicity, or have some other ulterior motive for coming forward with supernatural stories. Some people may even be emotionally troubled to the point of mental illness. On the other hand, you will meet people with genuine, real life supernatural experiences. It will be up to you to determine which stories are credible and worthy of a ghost hunt.

Questions For the Witness

Let the witness know ahead of time that they do not have to answer any question that makes them feel uncomfortable or any questions that they feel is too personal. Explain to the witness that the more information they provide the better your chances will be of finding out exactly what happened.

NOTE: If the answer is "YES" to any of the following Yes/No questions in this section make sure to get explanations, details and any other relevant information.

Initial Questions:
- How many witnesses were present?
- Where did the sighting occur?
- What was the exact date?
- What was the exact time?

Condition Questions:
- What were the weather conditions like that day?
- What were the weather conditions like during the time of the sighting?
- Was there any visible lightning or did you hear thunder?
- Was there any form of precipitation? (Rain, snow, hail, fog, mist)
- Was there any kind of electrical problems before, during or after the sighting?
- Was there any kind of temperature variation before, during or after the sighting?

Apparition Questions:
- Can you describe the apparition?
- How far away from the apparition were you?
- Did the apparition cast a shadow?
- Did the apparition manipulate or move any objects?
- Did the apparition make eye contact with you?
- Did the apparition acknowledge your presence in any way?
- Did the apparition speak to you? If yes, what exactly did it say?
- Did the apparition move? If yes, explain.
- Could you see through the apparition?
- Was the apparition wearing clothes?
- How long was the apparition visible?

Witness Questions:
- Were you sleeping before the sighting?
- Were you tired before the sighting?
- Did you call out for help or scream during the sighting?
- Did you recognize the apparition?
- Did you attempt to speak to or communicate with the apparition?
- Were you able to shoot a picture or video of the apparition?
- Did you attempt to move closer to the apparition?
- What do you believe happened?
- Have you ever experienced anything similar before?
- Do you know of anyone that has experienced anything similar?

General Questions:

- Where there any animals present at the time of the sighting?
- What were the reactions of the animals?
- How did the animals act during the course of that day?
- How did the animals act after the sighting?
- Did any objects break before, during, or after the sighting?
- Was there a physical or sexual attack by the apparition?
- Did you hear any abnormal sounds? What did they sound like?
- Did you hear any abnormal voices? What did they sound like or say?
- Did anything else unusual happen?

Residential Questions:

- What type of residence? (house, apartment, etc.)
- What type of structure? (brick, wood, stone, etc.)
- What is the construction date of the dwelling?
- What are the dimensions of the dwelling in square feet?
- What is the address?
- How many total rooms?
- How many bedrooms?
- Is there an attic and is it furnished?
- Is there a basement and is it furnished?
- Is there a garage? (1 car, 2 car, carport, etc.)
- Does the dwelling have property? Size?
- Is there a lake, pond, or natural water source on the property?
- Are there any other physical structures on the property?
- In which room(s) do the paranormal activities occur?
- Does any natural occurrence precede, or trigger paranormal activity?
- Have there ever been construction alterations or additions?
- Has there ever been a fire at the dwelling? List Damage and date.
- Does the basement flood?
- Have the dwelling's water pipes and/or electrical wiring ever been replaced?
- Have there been séances, or Ouija Boards used inside the dwelling?
- Have any blessing rituals or exorcisms been performed inside the dwelling?
- Has anyone ever died inside the dwelling?
- Has there been a death anywhere on the property?
- Has anyone ever been murdered inside the dwelling?
- Does the dwelling have a known history of violence?
- Is there any information on any former occupants?

Medical Questions:

- Did you consume alcohol in the last 24 hours before the sighting? When, what and how much?

- Did you take any prescription medication in the last 24 hours? When, what and how much?
- Did you take any over the counter medication in the last 24 hours? When, what and how much?
- Do you wear glasses or contact lenses? Were you wearing them at the time of the sighting?
- Have you ever been under psychiatric care?
- Have you ever been diagnosed as a schizophrenic?
- Do you have any known health problems?
- How is your sleep?
- Has your sleeping pattern changed?
- Are you getting a full night sleep?
- Have you had any nightmares lately?
- Have you been experiencing headaches, nausea, stomach pains, or dizziness?
- Have you vomited in the past 2 days?
- Have you ever had a Near Death Experience (NDE)?
- Are you currently seeing a medical doctor for anything?
- Do you feel depressed or nervous? If yes, explain.
- Do you feel you have abnormal amounts of stress or anxiety in your life?
- Has any member of your family recently died?

Personal Account:
- What were you doing at the time before the sighting occurred?
- What first made you notice the apparition?
- What did you think the apparition was when you saw it?
- Describe all of your actions during and after the apparition sighting.
- Describe all of the apparition's actions and reactions.
- How did you lose sight of the apparition?

Research Before the Ghost Hunt

Research makes up a majority of what ghost hunters do on a paranormal investigation. Good research will lead to more successful results in the field. Bad research, or no research, will leave a ghost hunter guessing, which always leads to failure. Developing intuitions and gut feelings are good, but let them come from knowing the facts through research. Prospective ghost hunters avoid research for one of three reasons. (1) They think that the word "research" means boring scientific work. (2) They don't know how or where to begin researching. (3) And finally, they do not understand that good research is easy to do and will aid them in any ghost hunt. If doing ghost-hunting research is boring, then you are not doing something right. A majority of the research is spent listening to people tell ghost stories. You will be reading through old newspaper articles that might expose some clues, stories about murders, suicides or tragic deaths. You'll also put together location histories including lists of all the people that live in a house and what their personalities were like when they were alive. Ghost hunters must consider themselves detectives on the search for the evidence and clues that will help them catch the ghost.

Begin the research by talking with neighbors. Find out if the neighbors know anything about the ghost, past occupants or any strange happenings. If you are looking for old newspaper articles, go to either the local library or the local newspaper. They both should have back issues of city newspapers on film for review. Some even have them in a computer database that will make your search easier by letting you enter key words. Newspapers should also have a research department. If you need structural records or names of past occupants, you can check the local library, the town hall, or the county courthouse. Some paranormal investigators feel intimidated about calling the courthouse or visiting City Hall because they are government run buildings. Those institutions are there to help the public and all of this information is public record. Give your local government offices a call and they will point you in the right direction. Another way to gain information may be through a title search company; however, they will charge you a fee. Of course, there is always the Internet. If you have no access to an Internet connection, you should be able to use a computer at your local library. Most are set up with free Internet access for the public.

There are so many ghost hunters and skeptics that go into a ghost hunt without doing any research. They spend a couple days at the haunted location and nothing happens so they label the case a hoax. If they would have spent a couple hours researching, they might have been able to turn up some useful information. Maybe the ghost only appears on the anniversary of its death. If the ghost hunter or skeptic does not have that information, then of course, they won't see or experience anything paranormal on a randomly chosen day. A good ghost hunter must try to determine what kind of ghost they are dealing with through research so that they will have a better chance of experiencing the paranormal.

Research is key for any good ghost hunter.

Developing a Spirit Profile

Ghost hunters want to see a ghost or experience something paranormal. You have a much better chance of experiencing the paranormal if you go the extra step and develop a spirit profile. This profile is really no different than what the FBI uses to track down criminals. If you want to catch something elusive, you have to understand its way of thinking. Profiling is a psychological process of getting into the "mind" of the ghost to uncover patterns of consistent behavior. This information will aid you in the ghost hunt by helping to determine what kind of spirit you are dealing with. Once you have that information, you should be able to make an educated guess as to when and where the paranormal activity is most likely to occur.

You first want to research the background of the ghost. Attempt to identify who the ghost was in life. Once they are identified, gather as much information on that person as possible. In the beginning, no detail should be considered too small. Never overlook or discount anything. Look for information about the suspected ghosts personality - were they married, did they smoke or drink, what was their favorite food, etc. Probably the most important questions: Did they have any special earthly attachments in life? What was the exact date of death? What was the cause of death? Interview people that may have known the person in life. Close friends, family, anyone that would have information that you could not collect in archives. Sometimes the ghost cannot be identified in the human form or the ghost is so old that there are no longer any living friends or relatives to interview. In those cases do the best you can.

Once the life history is finished, move on to identifying the characteristics of the ghost. Does the haunting activity stay in one particular location or room? Does the ghost make noises during a certain time of day? Do they move objects? If so, what objects? Do they ever manifest in apparition form? Do any of the haunting characteristics happen on specific days such as the anniversary of death? Again, nothing should be left out. Find out everything you can. Use local libraries and town records to do research and interview anyone that may have experienced this ghost in the past. Take every detail of a haunting into account and record everything. Once all the pieces of the haunting have been gathered, then you can analyze your notes looking for possible patterns. If you discover that the ghost appears more frequently on every third Sunday at 3 a.m. in the living room, then that is when and where you set up for a ghost hunt. If you find that the ghost moves objects in the children's room sometime in the middle of the night, then set up video cameras and conduct some kind of surveillance in that room at night. If the ghost manifests on the anniversary of its murder in the exact spot where the killing took place, then this is obviously where you should be on that day.

Spirit profiling is not hard. Simply write down everything that you can find out about the ghost through interviews and research and then analyze the facts. If you have enough information, consistent patterns begin to emerge. Many ghost hunters make the mistake of not doing any research and neglect to create a spirit profile. They go into a haunted location and spend a couple of days investigating. When nothing paranormal happens, they go back home disappointed. Had they spent some extra time doing a small amount of research, they would have had a much better chance of knowing exactly when and where to expect to experience a ghost.

The Fear Factor

Human fear plays a large role in ghost sightings and the experiences of a haunting. When people begin to believe that they have a ghost haunting their home, the natural fears involved push experiences along creating an environment where anything, no matter how logical, becomes something paranormal. People read about haunted houses and listen to what friends tell them even if the information is wrong. People living in a haunted house may begin "actively" participating in the haunting. When people listen closely for strange noises, any little sound becomes magnified. They will hear all kinds of natural noises that probably were always there, but went unnoticed. They will lay awake at night staring into the darkness of their rooms until their eyes finally see something: a dark apparition, a shadow moving, or an evil face looming back at them from the foot of their bed. The reality is that it's only their imagination and fears controlling what they "think" they are experiencing. The suggestion of a ghost or haunting is enough to cause people to expect to experience the paranormal.

Of course, this does not mean that there is no ghost or haunting occurring behind all the strange happenings, but it is important to understand that fear and the

human mind can involuntarily create an atmosphere of unnecessary terror. The truth is 99% of haunting cases are non-violent and non-intrusive. There is almost nothing to be afraid of. Most of the terror comes from a natural fear of the unknown, an instinctive method of human survival. Through education and understanding, we are able to realize that ghosts are not here to threaten us and in many of the cases, the ghosts seem unaware of the presence of living individuals. People who have learned to live with ghosts in their homes have described it as an enlightening spiritual experience.

Never try to communicate with ghosts by means of séances or Ouija boards. If you have something to say to the ghosts, simply say it out loud to them. Many families living with ghosts say that if they ask nicely, the ghosts will respect almost any request.

Keep a journal of all events that are considered to be part of the haunting. Watch for anything out of the ordinary that could be considered violent. Take any violent or malevolent actions extremely serious. While haunts are not violent by nature, poltergeists can be violent. That is why it's very important to distinguish between the two. They both share some basic characteristics. The differences won't become apparent until the poltergeist moves further into its energy cycle.

Safety precautions are necessary for protection, especially if there are young children involved. Always think safety first!

Ghosts Captured on Film and Video

Concrete visual evidence of the existence of ghosts is only one important reason to try to capture the image of a ghost on film or video. The camera can be a cheap hand-me-down or a brand new state of the art model as long as it works properly. The basic rule is that all ghost hunters should own and carry a camera with them at all times. Don't get caught unprepared! One big question that ghost hunters usually have is, "what camera and film works best?" The answer will vary depending on whom you ask. There does not seem to be a special camera model more likely to film a ghost. A good recommendation is a 35mm camera with adjustable settings. Remember to always use brand new film.

Too many first time ghost hunters make the common mistake of waiting until they have an irregular equipment reading before taking a photograph. Photos should be taken almost constantly at the beginning, middle, and end of ghost hunts. This cannot be stressed enough - there is no such thing as too many pictures! Always carry emergency rolls of film just in case you run out and need more. Learn to manage your film and videotapes. The worse thing that can happen is that you run out of film or videotape half way through a ghost hunt. Also remember to bring along the extras like light meters, backup sets of batteries and pre-charged power cells for any cameras that require them. Don't forget tripods!

Digital cameras have exploded onto the ghost-hunting field in a major way and it's easy to see why. There is no cost for film and they literally have an endless amount of picture taking ability. Ironically, the biggest upside to the digital camera is also the biggest downside. Digital cameras do not use film; therefore, there are no negatives. Without negatives it is virtually impossible to prove that the pictures have not been manipulated. In this field, everything is considered fake until proven otherwise. Digital cameras are great money saving tools; just keep in mind that the pictures taken with them will not be considered hard evidence.

Spirit photos allow ghost hunters to examine the energy patterns of the ghost. Cameras have the ability to pick up spectrums of light that the human eye cannot register. A picture is worth a thousand words, but a picture of a ghost is worth a thousand theories. There are ghost hunters that claim some ghosts like to be photographed. In haunted house sessions, the ghost hunter asks out loud if the ghost would like to pose for a photograph. The ghost hunter proceeds to take several pictures of a room. Later when the film is developed, the ghost hunter has a nice set of ghost photos to show off. This process sounds crazy to some people, but there are ghost hunters who are doing it with success. Either way, it can't hurt to give it a try from time to time. You might turn up some shocking results.

You have to be very careful with any visual evidence that you collect. Make sure that all videotapes and film negatives are stored safely where they will not be damaged or stolen. A fireproof lock box is usually a good place. Do not lay videotapes near any electrical equipment or magnets because the electromagnetic pulses will damage the videotapes.

Make several copies of the video right away. You do not want to have to keep reviewing the original and run the risk of having a freak accident occurring like the VCR eating the tape. Make backups of everything, including film negatives.

Never give anyone the original copies of videotapes or film negatives, even if they claim to be sending the evidence to get an expert opinion. Consult a lawyer first. It's not as expensive as most people think. You need to make sure that the claims of professional examination are legitimate. The lawyer can arrange a contract between you and whomever you are giving or selling the evidence too. If you do not do this and your film or video "mysteriously" disappears, you will have very little legal recourse. Treat any visual evidence you collect as a winning million-dollar lottery ticket. Ghost hunters have to live on a double-edged sword when it comes to visual evidence. On one side responsible ghost hunters should be weary of individuals claiming to have ghostly evidence without the proper professional examination. Every piece of visual evidence has to undergo intense scrutiny until it can stand on its own. On the other hand, the ghost hunter must vigilantly defend ghostly evidence from the constant attacks of critics that come after it even after it is considered legitimate by the experts.

Critics Come from Every Direction

It is easy to see why critics of this field have had so many problems with spirit photography in the past. Spiritualists abused the public by constantly creating one fake ghost photograph after another. Fake photos were so bad that the quality was laughable at best. Out of literally thousands of alleged spirit photos taken this century, only a small handful of ghost photos have stood the test of time. The Brown Lady ghost photograph taken on September 19, 1936 in Raynham Hall, Norfolk, England by two photographers from Country Life Magazine shows a female apparition descending the stairs just before the figure disappeared. This photograph has been examined by countless experts and has been validated to be authentic. The photographers were well respected and professional and never profited from the photograph. No one has ever been able to provide any evidence that the photograph was a hoax or that the picture is some kind of natural anomaly. The Brown Lady photo is one of the few ghost photographs that has stood the test of time and the scrutiny of the world's harshest critics.

The same high tech equipment that ghost hunters have come to rely on in their investigations to prove the existence of ghosts is the same equipment that is being used by frauds to fake ghost sightings. There was a time when only very knowledgeable individuals with vast resources at their command could produce quality fakes. Now, anyone with a home computer can do it easily. Many ghost hunters do not like to believe it, but anyone, even a seasoned ghost hunter, can be fooled by a fake; and anything can be faked.

Fast computer systems with piles of memory, video input jacks and affordable editing software provides a fraud with the prefect environment to forge any piece of video footage, EVP recording or still photograph. Frauds can now create fakes that appear so legitimate that top experts in the field of photography and video analysis can been tricked. When there is no way to determine which sources are fakes and which are legitimate, then everything must be considered suspect.

Frauds seriously damage the entire supernatural investigation field and they must be uncovered and pointed out. The field of paranormal studies has come to the sad point where anyone that comes forward with evidence of the existence of ghosts is going to come under fire as a fraud. That aside, the visual evidence gathered in photos and video provides ghost hunters with a unique perspective into the supernatural world that cannot be gathered with eyewitness testimony or any other method of investigation. Amateur and professional ghost hunters have to push beyond criticism and strive for the visual evidence that their field is so desperately in need of. Do not worry about the hardcore cynics. No amount of evidence will ever be good enough for them. They obviously have ulterior motives involved in their science.

Questions about Photographs and Videotapes:

Here are some very important questions that should be asked about any video or photograph to uncover the frauds and help prove legitimate sources.

• Why was the photo or video taken in the first place?

This is a judgment call. Is there anything in the picture worth photographing in the first place? A picture taken from difficult angles or strange styles should also be considered a warning sign of a fraud unless a reasonable explanation exists.

• Are photo negatives or original videotapes available?

It is a real problem when the photographer has no film negatives or original videotapes. The evidence cannot be examined and tested by professionals. Be wary of a person that claims to have taken a ghost picture, but gives you the run around about providing the proper evidence.

• Are the owners of the camera, film or videotape willing to let experts examine them for any defects and natural or unnatural manipulations?

Experts can usually determine if the film negatives have been tampered with or if the equipment has any natural or unnatural defects causing irregularities that are being mistaken for something supernatural.

• What is the background of the photographer?

Are they in the computer or video field? Are they artists? Do they work in Hollywood? Are they writing a book based on their experiences? Are they making deals to sell their story? None of these career choices really matter when it comes to validity. People working in Hollywood, writers or video editors can see and photograph ghosts just like anyone else. However, personal backgrounds are important enough to take notice of for future reference.

Conclusions:

It may seem that parts of this section contradict each other. One paragraph tells you to not give out any visual evidence and another paragraph tells you to be wary of anyone that won't give out evidence. One paragraph condemns the critics and another paragraph tells you to thoroughly question anyone that claims to have evidence. When you are dealing with one-of-a-kind physical evidence, a delicate system of checks and balances exists from both sides. It may seem like a huge pain and a complete waste of time, but the system keeps everyone safe. If you choose not to follow it you may find yourself cheated and exploited.

EVP (Electronic Voice Phenomena)

The process of recording a spirit's voice on audiotape is referred to as EVP, or Electronic Voice Phenomena. It is a concept that has really caught on with ghost hunters.

The idea behind EVP: Go into an area that could contain paranormal entities and literally have a conversation with them. Ask them a question, wait a few seconds, and then ask another question. It is not important to actually hear the response to the questions. If you do hear a verbal response then your ghost hunt has just found gold. When you have finished asking all of your questions go back home and rewind the tape. You might want to record in short, one to five minute sessions and review the tape at the location. Listen carefully from the beginning to the end for anything out of the ordinary. It has been reported in some haunting cases that the ghosts have answered the questions. You have to listen closely, the answers are not always clear, and may even be in a different language.

There are now a large number of digital audio recorders on the market that drastically cut listening time and record much clearer than a cassette recorder. The voice activation systems on a regular cassette recorder will not pick up the first word spoken. This means if a ghost where to say two words such as, "good bye," the only thing recorded on a tape recorder would be the word, "bye." Digital audio recorders do not have that problem. Digital models record everything, including the first word. You won't miss anything. Digital audio recorders can save time and usually have several other helpful features that regular cassette recorders don't have such as file organizing systems, easy delete functions, backlit LCD readout screens, digital recording settings and recording light indicators.

Many ghost hunters have success with EVP recordings; however, there are some serious problems that need to be addressed. One key characteristic important with EVP is the ghost hunter's own listening process. The tapes have to be reviewed and carefully listened to several times. The problem is that if you listen to anything long enough you can begin to hear things. You also have to be able to weed out all the background noises such as passing cars, barking dogs, the wind, etc. There is also the power of suggestion. You may want to give the tapes to a trustworthy, impartial listener. Ghost hunters have the tendency to hear what they want to hear from the tapes. They know what questions were asked and have an idea of what answers to expect. The legitimacy of EVP recordings is impossible to prove, regardless of what is recorded. Critics have a valid point when they say that the sounds or voices recorded are either natural noises or hoaxes. There is no way to prove that they are wrong.

There are parapsychology theories that the ghostly voices being recorded on audio recorders are not necessarily the voices of the deceased. Some parapsychologists believe that the ghost hunters are using an unknown psychic ability to imprint the sounds and voices directly onto the recordings. Basically, the ghost hunter's thoughts are somehow being changed into an electric wave that only the audio recorders can pick up. However, there are a couple holes in this theory. There are instances where the voices recorded answer questions that the ghost hunter has no way of knowing at the time of the recording. It's only later, when the ghost hunter does research, that they discover that the ghost was correctly answering questions or had provided valid information.

Tips to Good EVP Recordings:

- Use a full size tape recorder, not the handheld models. The small tape recorders are fine for witness interviews but not for EVP recordings.
- Use an external, static free microphone.
- Always use brand new high quality tapes. Never record over old tapes. A chance always exists that the overlapping recordings will mix and you will hear things that should not be heard.
- Do not bump the microphone. If you do, make a verbal note of it on the tape. You may also want to note any other nature sounds such as gusting winds, creaking doors, etc.
- Don't take photos while holding the recorder in your hand. The sound of your camera may overlap with recorded ghost voices.
- Record in 20 to 30 minute sessions. You can record longer, but keep in mind that you have to listen to the tape later. If you record two hours of tape, then you have to listen to two hours of tape. That can be very time consuming.
- Ask clear and precise questions.
- Do not whisper during the recordings. You are not going to scare the ghosts away.

• After each question, wait at least 10 to 15 seconds before asking the next question. It won't do much good if you never let the ghost get a word in edgewise.

• Don't hold cameras or other pieces of equipment close to the recorders. There will be interference and sound distortions that can record overtop possible paranormal communications.

Anyone that wants to listen to EVP recordings made by other ghost hunters can find samples of them on the Internet. They are on almost every ghost hunting and paranormal Web Page. You can find them by searching for "EVP Ghost Recordings" on Internet search engines.

Where are the Ghosts?

Ghost hunters can usually find haunted locations by word of mouth. Once a location has been discovered, you can get the exact details by checking back issues of newspapers in the local library or with the local historical society. These places do not have to be old haunts. A haunting can begin the day after someone's death. It is important to get the dates and times of death because many ghosts appear on the anniversary of their passing.

Places of Mysterious, Violent or Untimely Deaths: This type of place could be in a spot on a battlefield or where a murder was committed. It could even be the middle of the road where a person was hit and killed by a car. There seems to be a connection between haunted locations and violent and untimely deaths.

Cemeteries and Graveyards: Tales of phantoms and ghostly appearances in cemeteries have been recorded in every culture of the world far back into history. Graveyards are good places to start a ghost hunt. Check local records for the gravesites of people that have been murdered or where people have seen ghosts in the past.

Old Buildings and Hotels: Try to find buildings that are more than one hundred years old. It's not a guarantee that it will be haunted, but the older the building the better chance you will have in finding some ghosts. If you can talk to someone that once worked there, you may find exactly what room to begin searching for ghosts.

Hospitals and Nursing Homes: What makes these haunting cases stand out is the fact that the witnesses to them are very credible individuals, usually doctors and professional nurses. The ghosts of deceased patients and phantom workers can be found haunting both hospitals and nursing homes. Most of these cases go untold because of strict administration policies about keeping silent. However, people talk and ghost stories are told. It will probably be impossible to get inside these places to conduct an official investigation.

Schools and Colleges: Almost every college campus has a ghost story or urban legend attached to it; some of these tales are worth checking into. Hot spots in schools include kitchens, gymnasiums and dorm rooms. Glowing ghosts have been seen floating across campuses such as Athens University in Ohio late at night from dorm room windows. There are over two hundred allegedly haunted schools in the United States alone.

Churches and Sanctuaries: Churches can surprisingly be some of the most haunted places a ghost hunter will ever find. There are old churches throughout England that report multiple ghosts. In Derbyshire, a headless woman materializes in the churchyard and a strange phantom parishioner. In Yorkshire, a figure in white materializes on a tombstone in the churchyard of St. Nicholas. Witnesses have seen the inside of the church illuminated with strange blue lights. Haunting activities in churches include candles lighting and flying around by themselves and strange blue glowing lights inside churches when no one is there.

Theaters and Museums: There can be ghosts of past employees; actors or even people that just came to the theater to watch shows. Asking around should dig up some stories. There is almost always a dressing room or balcony that no one goes into anymore because of strange happenings in the past.

Prisons and Concentration Camps: In prisons like Alcatraz, which is now closed, dozens of restless ghosts still occupy the cells. Slave camps and concentration camps are also sites where lingering spirits still appear. There is a connection between these haunts and places where groups of people were held together in pain and suffering.

Twenty Common Ghost Hunting Mistakes

Never do the following:

1. NEVER Trespass: Watch out for any posted warning signs. Always ask for permission before going onto someone else's property. Avoid all areas where access is prohibited. Trespassing will only get you thrown in jail or worse. Be careful.

2. NEVER Litter: Leave the area exactly as you found it. Pick up any trash, containers, and scraps of paper and tape. Wipe off any chalk marks unless the site is a secluded area and you plan on returning.

3. NEVER Go Alone: Have at least one partner on ghost hunts, even if the person

doesn't know anything about ghost hunting. This provides a little more safety and also a witness to any strange events that might occur. If you are alone and an unforeseen accident or emergency occurs, who will help?

4. NEVER Forget to Carry ID: If the police ever question you about being in a private location, you will need some form of picture identification, preferably a driver's license. The police do have the right to ask any citizen for an ID and, if you do not have one, they also have the right to detain you for questioning.

5. NEVER Forget to Tell People Where You Are Going: Tell someone where you will be at and how long you plan on being gone. If you run late in the ghost hunt, call and explain the situation. Never leave friends or loved ones wondering where you are.

6. NEVER Record False Equipment Readings: Test all of your equipment several times before leaving on an investigation. Replace batteries as needed. Learn to correctly use all of the equipment before even thinking about using them in the field. Remember to take background readings outside of the active site.

7. NEVER Go Directly to a Site at Night: Thoroughly check over the site in the daylight for any dangerous obstacles that may be invisible in the darkness.

8. NEVER Smoke, Drink Alcohol or Use Drugs: Do not impair your judgment or infect the site's environment with these substances. Use common sense.

9. NEVER Wear Colognes, Aftershave, or Perfumes: Never wear anything that creates a noticeable odor. The smells may affect other ghost hunter's judgments. The air needs to be clear to detect any abnormal odors. Some outside ghost hunts may require mosquito repellants. Use odor free bug sprays and log their use.

10. NEVER Forget to Carry a Notebook: Everything needs to be recorded and logged. No detail is too small. Keep lists of events, actions and times. Record with audio and video if possible.

11. NEVER Forget to Wear a Watch: This goes along with the logbook. You cannot record times if you do not know what time it is.

12. NEVER Whisper: Always speak clearly, especially if you are recording the ghost hunt. You do not want to later confuse your whispering as something supernatural. If there are ghosts around your voice is not going to scare them off.

13. NEVER Forget to do Research and Profiles: Too many ghost hunters neglect to do the proper research before going out into the field. What they fail to understand is that

good research will only help them with the possibilities of seeing a ghost.

14. NEVER Use a Car's Headlights as a Main Source of Light: Sometimes headlights come in handy for setting up campsites or equipment, but do not use them as a long-term light source. You could drain the battery enough that the car will not start.

15. NEVER Try to Bring Everything: Don't try to carry along every piece of equipment. Just bring the basics and the equipment that you absolutely need. Getting bogged down will only take your attention away from the ghost hunt.

16. NEVER Forget to Bring Flashlights: Always have plenty of working flashlights. Everyone should have two flashlights on hand.

17. NEVER Forget Extra Batteries: Know what kind of batteries each piece of equipment takes and how to change them. Always carry extra sets of batteries.

18. NEVER Forget to Take Lots of Pictures: Take as many photographs as you can. That goes the same for video. You cannot have enough of either. Just keep an eye on your film supplies. Do not run out before the ghost hunt is over. Always have emergency rolls of film.

19. NEVER Forget to Bring Food and Drinks: It may sound trivial, but you would be surprised how many ghost-hunts have been ruined or have been cut short because of the lack of snacks.

20. NEVER Go into Physically Dangerous Locations: It may be tempting to conduct ghost hunts in old condemned buildings or on the edge of a spooky cliff side, but avoid dangerous situations. The risk is simply not worth it. Also, never go to any place when the weather conditions are bad. Ghost hunts are meant to be fun and it will not be fun if someone gets hurt, has to go to the hospital or worse.

Publishing Work

The last step in all ghost hunts is providing the public with the findings of your investigation, your theories and final conclusions. Final reports should always be typed up with the proper title, headings and correct spelling and grammar. The format can vary. It is important that you use clear-cut statements that coincide with the evidence. The key word in publishing your work is "thoroughness."

You want to begin by providing the basic case and story background. Explain how this case came to your attention. Did you read about it? Did someone contact you? Was this an experience that you had? Once you've covered the necessary background information, move on to discuss any initial interviews, ghost stories or folklore tales. This is all part of setting up the story.

Next, begin to explain your methods of research in the ghost hunt. Did you find old newspaper articles of relevance? Did you put together a complete list of all the past owners and occupants? Did you find any other witnesses to collaborate or compare stories to? Where did you find this information? Did you check out the sources to make sure they were valid?

After explaining your research move into your theories about the case. It does not matter if you thought the case of natural or supernatural origin. What do you believe happened? What are your thoughts on the matter? Do you have any ideas about who the ghost was in life? Do you believe that this ghost only appears on certain nights or at certain times? Do you believe the noises heard in the attic were only raccoons sneaking in from outside at night? Tell us what you think is happening.

You need to back up your theories with the evidence that was discovered during the course of the investigation. If you believe that this ghost only appears one night a year can you explain why? Did they commit suicide on that day? Were they murdered in that spot? Do all the other witness sightings occur on that same day? You have to provide evidence to back up what you are saying. If you have no evidence then your theories are worthless. If you say that the ghost only appears on one day a year, but there are witnesses that say they saw the ghost on other days, then your theory doesn't hold.

Finally, move on to your conclusions. What do you think will happen in the future with this case? What kind of ghost is it? Will the sightings continue? What are your recommendations to the people living in the home? Do you believe that there is any way to end this haunting or send this spirit on to a more peaceful existence? Is this a real haunting? Are the ghosts real? Or is this something with a natural explanation?

The final conclusions should be based on your theories combined with the evidence that you have gathered to support those theories. Of course, there will be times when you have very good witness testimony and you feel comfortable about your theories, but enough hard evidence is not available to thoroughly support any conclusions. Do not make guesses. Your final conclusions must not be guesses. They should be based on facts. Leave the cases open if you cannot find enough evidence to support a solid conclusion. There may be a day in the future when more information becomes available. There is nothing wrong with not having an absolute conclusion or with leaving a case open.

Include a sheet somewhere in your file filled with possible natural causes: gusting wind, bad wiring, wild animals, etc. Fill in exactly what you did to explore each of those natural cases. If there are strange noises coming from inside a wall, people are going to ask if there are water pipes running through that wall or if there any holes that small animals might be able to crawl inside. Did you check the pipes? Did you check for any signs of animals? If so, list them.

Everything is finished, now what? Who do you give your published work too? Just about anyone that wants to look at it! Keeping your finished work a secret only leads to suspicions about you and your real motives. You may want to publish your work as a book or write an article about it for a magazine. You might also want to publish your ghost hunts on the Internet.

It's a good idea to share your results with other ghost hunters. They might be able to point out any investigation flaws. If there is a hole in your work, just go back and patch it up. Then, redo your final report taking any errors into account. If you hand over a finished report to a science or news organization that is riddled with mistakes, they will be more than happy to laugh in your face. Skeptics will attack your work from every angle and you will quickly be discredited. It is true that everyone makes mistakes and no investigation is flawless, but thoroughness in your methods and conclusions will mean more than you can ever imagine.

Quick Review:

1. Always spell check everything. Have the reports neatly typed out.
2. Do not use a bunch of scientific jargon. It will only confuse most people. Keep the wording simple. Write the final report as if you were talking to someone.
3. Keep your points short and to the point. Do not draw out long stories trying to include every single detail. If people have questions, let them ask.
4. Make sure to include all of the evidence. You cannot discount a piece of evidence simply because it seems to be the oddball that does not fit with your theories.
5. Follow up on cases from time to time, even when your cases have solid conclusions and good evidence. See if anything has changed over the years or if anything new is now happening in the case.
6. Have several copies of your notes, interviews, reports, recordings and pieces of evidence available for independent reviews.

Selling Work

Every ghost hunter will have a different opinion when it comes to selling stories or pieces of evidence such as pictures or videos. Some say that it diminishes the credibility of the field when something is sold and used for profit. Others will say that there is nothing wrong with making money from your own hard work. The bottom line is that it is really up to you. Do what you feel like doing.

Selling stories is usually the main source of income for a ghost hunter. Ghost hunting is primarily a part time job or a hobby for many that take part in the field. Almost all ghost hunters have other full time jobs that have nothing to do with hunting ghosts. A stable income and extra money are important to everyone and some of those high tech ghost-hunting gadgets don't come cheap.

The main source of money being made by ghost hunters comes from books. Ghost hunters write books about their cases or field methods. Some compile lots of stories into one book or focus on a certain type of ghost or haunting. Paranormal books are very popular and they can make you some good extra money.

There are a couple of ways to get your book published. First make sure that you have a fully completed manuscript. It must be cleaned up, error free and ready to go. You can either contact the publishers directly or go through a literary agent. Literary agents will take a percentage of your profit, but many publishers would rather deal with them rather than you simply because they know the business. A plus to literary agents is that they tend to get you a better deal because they do know the business. However, if you feel comfortable with making your own deals or know a little about the book publishing business then bypass the literary agent altogether. Always check the references of agents, publishers and printers. Contact the Better Business Bureau and shop around to find the best deals.

Do not get down on yourself if your manuscript constantly gets rejected. Don't stop trying to sell it. Rejection does not mean that your work is not good. A lot of big time writers were turned down thirty or more times before getting their number one best seller published. The nature of the book business is to be turned down. Even if you cannot find a publisher or agent that will take your work you still have options. You may want to self-publish your own book. You can do this a couple different ways. You can either pay a publisher to have your book printed or you can become the publisher and hire a printer to print and bind your book. There are upsides and downsides to self-publishing. One upside is that you get to keep all the profits that usually go to the publisher, which will add up very quickly. A downside to self-publishing is that you are now responsible for marketing and distributing your book.

You can also choose to sell your pictures to magazines or market your own line of videotape to make extra cash. You should be very careful about turning over any sample pictures or videotapes to media sources without first getting a deal in writing. You need to have a contract in writing that shows exactly how much you are supposed to be paid and when you are to be paid. Make sure that you retain full ownership and copyrights for anything that you give out. Make sure that you know exactly where and when the materials are going to be used and for what purpose they are to be used. Make sure that you get royalty fees included so that when your pictures or videotapes are used more than once, you get monetary compensation each time. It is not always important to receive a lot of money, but your time and work should be reasonably compensated in some manner. Do not be afraid to ask for something that you want or try to make deals. Whenever possible, get all of your money up front.

All of these methods of product marketing are much easier than they were in the past with the help of the Internet. You can setup a website for almost nothing and start promoting your product to a worldwide audience. If you need help there are consultants and self help books that you can get at a local library or bookstore about self-publishing, marketing strategies, and Internet web page design, setup and marketing. If you want to sell your work, then sell away. The only real problem is making sure that you get what you deserve and don't get ripped off in the process.

Never give up ownership rights to anything unless you are properly compensated. A lawyer may need to be consulted in these matters. Most lawyer consulting fees range from $20 to $40, which is a small price to pay for good legal advice.

Step-by-Step Ghost Hunting: A Quick Review

1. You hear or find out about a possible ghost.

2. First, conduct an interview with all of the witnesses. Get the facts and stories.

3. Proceed to the site with a minimal amount of ghost hunting equipment. (Notebook, EMF detector, still and video cameras). Look for any dangerous obstacles. Map out the area. Take notes.

4. Conduct a follow up interview with the witnesses. Verify story facts and ask any questions that you might now have after visiting the site. Find out if the witnesses are willing to conduct a reenactment. If they are, precede with the reenactment. Videotape the entire reenactment if possible.

5. Begin researching. Get records, conduct outside interviews with neighbors and others who have had supernatural experiences, find newspaper articles, do spirit profiles, make lists of past occupants, and dig up folklore and other ghost stories.

6. Conduct the first ghost hunt. Use all the necessary equipment and record the entire event.

7. Review your work. Go back and study each of your steps. Did you do everything correctly? Did you find all the information that you could? Is your research valid? If you do find a mistake in your work try to determine how it affected the outcome up to this point.

8. Do a second, third, and fourth ghost hunt. Conduct as many ghost hunts as needed to gather the physical evidence required to complete your investigation.

9. Complete a third follow up witness interview. Has anything in the witness's story changed over the course of the investigation? Did they remember anything new? Has anything new happened to them since the beginning of the investigation, any new sightings?

10. Begin work on a final written report. Include stories, facts, evidence, theories, conclusions and any other information prudent to the final report. There may not be enough evidence to make a valid conclusion; do not make up something. Leave the case open for future study.

11. Double and triple check all of these steps and your work involved in them. Look for any area of your investigation that could be considered incomplete and then go back and do your best to fill in that area. Have you done as much as possible in this ghost hunt?

12. Publish your results. Make sure to get full permission before using real names and stories. Always include copies of all your evidence and findings so that it can be thoroughly reviewed. Be prepared to defend the discoveries and conclusions of your investigation.

What Ghost Hunters Should Know

The Reasons for Ghosts

To understand the nature of ghosts, we must try to find the cause, meaning, and origin behind each ghost. If this fantastic afterlife exists for waiting souls beyond this world, a beautiful peaceful paradise, then why would some souls choose to stay on Earth? Do they even have a choice or are they stuck in a form of limbo? These are difficult questions to answer. No one particular reason stands out as to why the deceased linger in the world of the living. A majority of all ghost sightings and haunting cases have similar backgrounds. From an observational standpoint, the cause for ghosts seems to be directly linked to an event that happened in their lifetime.

Tragic, mysterious, violent, and untimely deaths are main triggers for a haunting. Unexpected deaths are just the first layer of this multi layer problem. An untimely death uncovers the powerful emotions of an unfinished life, an imprint of all the things that were left behind. The plans, the dreams, all of the gifts of life are gone without a moment's notice. The future is what we strive for in life. When that future is cut short, souls can be left confused and lost. Some souls might return to the Earth as ghosts and try to fulfill those lost futures. In death we leave loved ones behind, people that we are not ready to give up. Tragic events take soul mates from each other causing them to forever search for the one they miss. Some ghosts return searching for these loved ones, maybe to say a final goodbye or to close a door that was left open at the time of their passing.

There are individuals with a tremendous love of life. To them, death is a complete shock. These souls seem to refuse to let go of life. They refuse to go off to the other side and instead remain here on earth frequenting fond places from their life. They can be detected by the living from the presence of their favorite smells: perfumes, after-shave, cigar smoke, or fresh flowers. We can feel them sitting next to us or watching over us.

Almost all haunts are in places that the deceased knew in life. If ghosts have the ability to go anywhere in the world and do virtually anything, then why would these souls choose to come back to the same locations and reenact the same earthly chores that they more than likely complained about when they were still alive?

There are ghosts that don't seem to know they are dead. Whether this is by choice or some uncontrollable circumstance remains a mystery. Even though they are no longer alive, these ghosts continuously go through their daily routines as if nothing has ever changed. They are transfixed in a life that no longer exists, except to them. Understanding why ghosts are ghosts is very important in ghost hunting. When we break down the circumstances behind the existence of each ghost, a pattern begins to unfold. If ghost hunting teaches us anything, it should be that life is something special.

Getting Rid of Ghosts

When people find out that they have a ghost living in their house a common response is usually, "how can I get rid of it?" For centuries people have been coming up with different ways to force ghosts out or to prevent them from entering in the first place. Generally speaking, almost all of these methods are nothing more than home remedies passed down from generation to generation. The truth is, almost nothing can be done to chase a ghost away. The ghosts were usually there first and regardless of what magic the living conjures up, the ghost will still be there long afterwards. Some charms may seem to have an affect, but only suspend the haunting for a period. After a little time passes, the haunting symptoms return. If anything, the effects of the method seem to be more of a psychological effect on the person deploying the method.

These are some of the most common methods used to ward off unwanted ghosts.

Amulets: Amulets are objects that are believed to have the power of protection, good luck and defense against evil forces. Just about anything can be used as an amulet: jewelry, jewels, magic pouches, parchments, pieces of metal, knives, and religious symbols are some of the more popular amulets used. They are typically worn around the neck or carried somewhere on the body. Amulets can be placed inside homes, above doorways, in bedrooms, in burial tombs, and in holy places. It is believed by some that amulets will stop diseases, bad luck, and misfortune for the person carrying the amulet. The main use for the amulet through out history was to counter the effects of evil spirits and to ward off unwanted ghosts. The Babylonians and Syrians used cylinder seals, which were imbedded with precious stones. The Hebrews wore crescent moons to ward off evil spirits. The natives of Africa carry amulets consisting of a pouch of fruits, plants, or vegetables. Egyptian amulets could be massive in size such as the stone beetle mounted on a pedestal at Karnak measuring five feet long by three feet wide and weighing more than two tons.

Talisman: Talismans are objects that give their owners magical or supernatural powers. These powers can be used to combat the effects of ghosts and evil spirits. There are talismans that are believed to give their holder power to command the spirits of the dead. Occult folklore says that talismans can also attract luck, health, success, love, happiness, and power. The power of each talisman can come from one of three sources: from nature, from God, or from supernatural entities. Talismans should not be confused with amulets. Amulets ward off bad energies. Talismans attract good energy and give magic powers.

Charms: Charms are special concoctions made from natural ingredients intended to bring good luck and ward off evil spirits. They are usually put into a pouch to be worn or carried. There are some charms that can be worn like a perfume or makeup. Most of the charms made have a powerfully strong odor to them. The charms can be made from natural elements such as garlic, sage, clover, etc. The elements are stewed or ground together into a powder or paste. Charms can include four leaf clovers, personal ornaments, jewelry, necklaces, horseshoes and even lucky rocks.

Salt: Salt is a remedy used to hold evil spirits at bay. A little bit of salt poured or spread in areas of a home, such as doorways and windowsills, is said to block out evil spirits from entering or crossing over the lines of salt. The salt can be spread in a circle, typically referred to as a circle of protection. Anyone standing inside the ring of salt will be safe from evil spirits. Ghosts and evil spirits have to stay on the outside of the salt circle. Salt can be carried in pockets for luck and to ward off lingering spirits.

Silver: Silver is another element used to keep away ghosts and evil spirits. It is considered to be a metallic element of purity and has been used for protection against evil in almost every world culture throughout history such as the Sumerians, Egyptians, and Mongolians. Silver can be melted down to form amulets, jewelry, bullets, daggers, and religious symbols such as crucifixes. Silver amulets and daggers can be put into the ground above the grave to prevent the ghost from escaping. Silver nails driven into coffin lids are said to help prevent ghosts. It is a belief that the chemical element silver holds certain powers that can enhance human psychic abilities. And, of course, most people know the folklore legend that silver bullets kill werewolves.

Exorcism: Exorcism is a religious rite preformed by holy men to cast out ghosts, evil spirits, and demons from either the human body or location. The exorcism ceremony is complex and dangerous. Only trained professionals should try to perform them. They usually consist of diligent praying, continuous readings of Bible passages or sacred writings, ritual blessings, and the spreading of holy water and religious symbols. Exorcists need to have intense, unshakable religious belief plus the physical abilities needed to continue the exorcism rites day and night for as long as is needed. Exorcisms have been known to last for days, months, and even years. In 1949 an evil spirit possessed a then thirteen-year-old boy named John Hoffman. As the boy's condition worsened, the Roman Catholic Church stepped in and began to perform the Right of Exorcism. The Church documented the case for the next several months. Details include objects in the room moving and levitating. The boy could speak in other languages and could respond correctly to languages that he had no way of ever knowing. Strange scratch marks and words would randomly appear on the boy's skin. The boy's body was ravaged with violent spasms. The possession lasted for nearly five months before the spirit was successfully exorcised. A writer named William Peter Blatty picked up on the story and wrote a best selling book based loosely on the boy's experience in 1971 called *The Exorcist.*

Blessing: A minister, priest, or a holy man can use various prayers and blessings that can ward off ghosts. Prayers, chanting, and religious symbols spread throughout a home are supposed to help in freeing the house from ghosts and spirits. Praying for the soul of the deceased spirit still lingering in the home is said to sometimes work. There are numerous blessing prayers that can be used.

Prayer: Various religious prayers are said to help get rid of unwanted ghosts and evil spirits. The only catch with this tool is its effectiveness. The crucifix (or any other religious artifact) and the prayer are only as strong as a person's faith. The person reciting the prayer must completely believe in what they are saying in order for it to have any affect.

Ask the Ghost Yourself: It sounds strange, but there have been cases where people living with ghosts have just asked the ghosts not to appear or cause any problems when they are around and it has worked. It could save you a lot of time and money and in the long run it can't hurt to give it a try. Simply stand in the room where you believe the ghost to be the most active and polity request that it stop doing whatever it is that is bothering you and your family.

The So Called Ghost Buster: There are people out in the world that claim to be able to get rid of ghosts using equipment like high tech electromagnets, electromagnetic pulse generators, and air ion distorters. You should use a great deal of caution before bringing these people into your home. Some of them may be very credible and honest people who are really trying to rid your home of ghosts, but others will be nothing more than con artists looking for an easy way to make a fast buck. Ask a lot of questions. Always get and check references. Never pay in cash. Never pay up front. Never pay large sums of money for the job. Find out if they offer a money back guarantee on their work.

Psychics: The psychic business can be even shadier than the ghost busters. Psychics can come into your home and make up elaborate stories about the ghosts. They get paid a lot of money for their services and, more often then not, will leave you stuck with the same ghost problem. There are credible psychics in the world. The problem is that they are very rare. The same rules of protection apply. Ask questions. Get references. Never pay in cash. Never pay up front. Never pay a lot of money. Keep in mind that even the world's best psychic really has no power over ghosts. They may be able to explain who the ghost is and why they are here, but there is no guarantee that they can make the ghosts do anything that they don't want to do.

Gargoyle Statues: Legends say that gargoyle statues ward off evil spirits. These statues are usually fashioned from cement, resin, and plaster. Gargoyles were initially created as sculptural spouts that would direct rainwater away from the walls of medieval cathedrals. Minster Cathedral in York, England, the Washington National Cathedral in Washington DC, and New York Carver Cathedrals all don gargoyle statues. Gargoyles got their name from the gurgling sounds that the water make when shooting off of them. The gruesome appearance of the Gargoyle statue also kept superstitious thieves away. As time went on, rumors began to circulate that the gargoyles were breaking out of their stone structures and flying off into the evening sky. Before morning, they would return to their perch high on top of the gothic cathedrals and return to stone until the next night.

Placing of Religious Symbols: Believers say that placing meaningful religious symbols in all of the rooms of your home will keep ghosts and evil spirits out. These symbols can be Bibles, small statues of saints, angels, or religious pictures. These symbols must have a spiritual significance to you personally or the items will be worthless. It is not the symbols so much as it is the faith that you have for them. The religion you serve does not seem to matter. For example, several academy parapsychology experiments have been done over the past decade with people of different religious faiths, (Christianity, Judaism, Buddhism), where each have placed artifacts from their own religious faiths in rooms thought to be haunted and the haunting activity has stopped.

Recording Orbs

Many paranormal investigators believe that orbs are the essence of the soul or "life-force" left behind after death. Orbs are perfect circles of pure energy that can be photographed and videotaped but almost never seen with the naked eye. Floating orbs retain a conscience with the same emotions, intelligence and personality traits of the living individual it represents. These orbs will sometimes respond to human communication with a cause and effect relationship; meaning that paranormal investigators will ask the ghosts to do something, (appear, disappear, multiply or manifest in a particular location), and the orbs will respond in kind.

Clusters of dust particles or rain droplets will be reflected in the flash of a camera falsely appearing as orbs. It is important to know the conditions of the location you are photographing. Walking in a dusty area can kick up enough dust into the air to cause false orb anomalies to appear in photographs. Moisture on the camera lens or in the air can cause false orbs and other strange effects.

Lens Flares can also be mistaken for ghostly orbs. The flares appear as six sided shapes with circular balls of light streaming through them. Lens flare orbs travel in a direct line from the path of the sun to the photographer. Photographs at night can obviously not have sunlight flares, but any bright light can cause a lens flare to occur.

Spider webs or cobwebs, cigarette smoke, insects, fog, snow, and moisture condensation can also create common false photographic orbs. Never take photographs in rain or snowfalls. If the weather conditions are cold, watch that your exhaled breathe does not pass in front of the camera.

The flash on most cameras will only be useful for the first fifteen to twenty-five feet. Any orbs beyond your camera's flash range will not appear in the photograph. Make sure to keep the camera lens clean and free of any dirt or hairs. Fingers and camera straps can also be a problem. Keep all fingers away from the front of the camera and keep the camera straps pulled back or remove them.

The Heart of a Haunting

The term *heart* refers to a precise location where paranormal activity occurs with the most frequency. The heart is the nucleus of the paranormal phenomena. If a paranormal investigator can discover why the heart is the focal point of the paranormal energy, then they will unlock the secrets to the source of the haunting. Hearts are the power center of paranormal activity. As the invisible perimeter expands outward in a circular pattern away from the heart, the paranormal activity will slowly decrease. The stronger the heart, the larger and stronger the perimeter circle of paranormal activity will be.

Haunted locations can have more than one heart. To quote the movie *Poltergeist*, "This house has many hearts." The cause of a heart can vary widely from a murder scene to a favorite room. Each heart will have a different underlying cause. It is an important job of the paranormal investigator to discover the location of the heart and to determine why each heart is the focus of the paranormal activity.

Hearts can sometimes be referred to as "hot spots." It is important not to confuse these "hot spots" with the description of physical locations that have above average temperatures without cause or explanation.

Spirit Burns

(Sometimes referred to more correctly as a *Psychic Burn.*)

A Spirit Burn is a location where a terrible event, typically extremely violent, occurs causing human emotions, (fear, panic, anger, pain, hate, confusion, etc.), to explode from the scene like a psychic atomic bomb scarring the physical environment. A Spirit Burn is a forced imprint that acts in ways very similar to a typical haunting. Visitors to these areas will experience loud noises, shadowy apparitions, screams, bellowing cries, and ghostly reenactments. Spirit burned locations can be very powerful sites, drawing negative energy to them as a magnet. Visitors can experience feelings of painful human emotions without cause. The Spirit Burned area seems to be able to draw the emotional energy from living visitors into its own psychic structure. It does not appear that Spirit Burns are the result of ghosts or spirits and work independently of other paranormal and supernatural controls. Because of their violent traumatizing nature, Spirit Burns are widely mistaken for sites of demonic activity.

Spirit Burns should not be looked at as a haunted location, but instead as a site where pure psychic energy has massed tightly together in a chaotic, fluctuating state. While the actions of Spirit Burned sites may appear to be under intelligent control, they are actually completely random events. Spirit Burns are concentrated to one solid location. They are confined to the exact size of the violent incident that caused the Spirit Burn to occur. There will not be any other paranormal activity outside of this confined location.

Awakenings

An *awakening* is the exact moment when paranormal activity suddenly and unexpectedly emerges from a location where no paranormal activity has ever been reported or has not been reported in a long period of time. The increasing ghostly activity usually begins in a previously dormant location as a result of human interference. When the living (knowingly or unknowingly) infringe upon the territory of a dormant ghost, there can be dramatic paranormal increases and psychic transformations.

Locations undergoing structural alterations such as old hotels, ballrooms, churches, theaters, hospitals, and construction sites are the most common locations to experience an awakening. Vacant land construction over unknown burial ground, holy ground, and other sacred sites can also set off an awakening.

Spirit awakenings differ slightly from a typical ghost haunting. The psychic energies involved with an awakening are similar to the energies of a poltergeist. The paranormal activities will increase over time from almost unnoticeable events to terrifying and violent actions. The initial phase of an awakening will be obscure. The paranormal events will resemble a classic haunting; construction tools or personal objects will disappear or relocate to other areas of the workplace. Strange noises, unidentifiable voices, whispering, and footsteps are frequently early characteristics of an awakening. As time passes, and if the ghost's subtle requests for peace are not heeded, the disturbances will increase until reaching sometimes violent levels. Heavy objects fall dangerously close to people at the worksite. Perfectly functioning electrical equipment will suddenly fail or super charge without explanation at key moments that could cause harm. Unseen forces turn on water pipes to flood certain areas, and mysterious fires start up for no reason. The awakening experience can be extremely terrifying, and even life threatening for any anyone who happens to come in contact with this type of paranormal activity.

The time frame of an awakening will vary. In some cases, the paranormal activity will cease the very moment that outside intrusions have stopped or when construction work is completed. The paranormal activity can pick back up if future intrusions are made on the location. On the other hand, there are some awakenings where the paranormal activity has continued on indefinitely.

What to do if you see a Ghost

Seeing a ghost is a once in a lifetime opportunity. If you are lucky enough to find yourself face to face with a ghostly apparition, you should attempt to take full advantage of the situation. You may never get this chance again.

Fear is always the first reaction to seeing a ghost. It is a common, natural, human expression. Everyone that comes in contact with a paranormal entity will be afraid. The key is trying to keep your fear from turning into panic. Try to remain calm. Of course this is easier said than done, but it is necessary to take full advantage of the experience.

Most ghost sightings only last for a hand full of seconds. It is important to take full advantage of the time that you have to study the description and actions of the ghost. Take mental notes, can you see through the ghost? What kind of clothes is the ghost wearing? Is the ghost male or female? How old does the ghost look? Is the ghost floating? Is it a full apparition or are there parts like legs missing? Watch the ghost closely. What is it doing? Is it manipulating either ghostly objects or real objects? Examine the ghost and try to remember everything about it that you can. The information is vital when determining what type of ghost you are dealing with.

After you examine the ghost for a moment, try to communicate with it. Start by saying hello or by giving it your name. You might try taking a small step toward the ghost. See if the ghost notices or acknowledges your presence. The ghost may look up or make eye contact. If it does, stop moving and try to talk with it. Speak clearly in a regular tone. You don't have to shout.

If you happen to have a camera nearby, grab it and try to get some pictures before the apparition vanishes. Remember you may only get one opportunity at this in a lifetime. Do everything that you can to gather visual evidence of the ghost.

Any communication with a ghost makes it possible for a ghost hunter to conclude that this ghost is not an Atmospheric Apparition. Atmospheric Apparitions are not ghosts, but instead believed to be past events that have somehow imprinted themselves onto the environment and continuously replay.

Keep your eyes on the ghost until you lose sight of it. If the ghost wanders off into another room, slowly follow it. Try to find out where it is going. Everything that the ghost does is a clue into the insight of that ghost. Does the ghost dissolve into thin air? Does it go into another room only to vanish? Does it disappear by going through a wall?

As soon as the experience is over, you need to sit down and write out everything. Answer all of the **Questions For the Witness** in the **Methods of a Ghost Hunt** chapter.

What to do if Your House is Haunted

If you believe that your house is haunted, there are some things that you can do. First, get yourself a notebook and keep a written journal of every single event that occurs. Also, keep notes on what you have done to find the sources of the strange events. For example, if you are hearing noises coming from your basement, you check out the water pipes and find no problems with them then make a note of that.

You can also try doing some EVP audio recordings. Walk around the house with a tape recorder and a microphone and make recordings. Ask questions to the ghost as you go. Then, rewind the tape and listen to it. See if there are any strange sounds or voices recorded on the tape. These could be the voices of the ghosts responding to your questions.

Do research. Get a list of all of the past owners. Find out if any of the past owners or anyone else has ever died inside your home. You can get some of this information by going to the local courthouse. There you will find a copy of the deed to the house. Neighbors may also be able to provide you with some information. Ask them if they have ever heard or seen anything out of the ordinary in the past.

If the haunting activity seems to be concentrated to a single area of your house, maybe one room, try setting up a video camera and let it run during the times when the haunting activity seems most active. Later, go back and watch the videotape. You may discover something paranormal on the tape or you may find something completely natural behind the strange phenomena. People who have tried this experiment have turned up some malicious little culprits to their haunts that include wild animals, children who have decided to fake a ghost, and even household pets running wild.

Take photographs in all the rooms of your house. For best results use a 35mm camera with a brand new roll of film. There are ghosts that will only turn up on photos. The pictures you take may reveal a ghostly face or a blurred area on the picture. Energy bulbs and round circles of white light called orbs have been photographed. If you do take pictures throughout your house only to discover that all of the pictures came out looking normal, this does not mean that you definitely do not have a ghost. Of course, the same goes for any pictures that you see smears or smudges on. It is not a definite sign of ghosts, but it is one more piece of circumstantial evidence.

You have to consistently make valid efforts to identify the things that are happening in a rational manner, like strange noises or electrical problems. Check around the outside edges of your house. Look for ways that wild animals could be sneaking into your home. Check all the windows to make sure that they are firmly sealed. If you are having electrical problems, call in an electrician to check the wiring. Be rational and thorough. Go through every scenario that might be able to produce or duplicate the same phenomena that you are experiencing. Most of the time, people discover that the causes of the haunting are actually down to earth occurrences.

If you have gone through and checked every detail to the best of your abilities and are not satisfied, you can always try bringing in a psychic. The only problem with getting a psychic is finding an honest psychic. Don't pay a lot of money for their services. Ask around. You may even get lucky and find a credible psychic that will not charge you any money. Do not be afraid to ask for references and do not be afraid to pit psychic against psychic. Bringing in two different psychics may help you weed out the fakes or, at least, make their prices more competitive. You should only call a psychic after you have done all the other steps. That way, you will have the necessary background information and will be able to tell right away if the psychic is genuine or simply making up details as they go.

Ghost Hunting is Dangerous!

Many people ask if ghost hunting is dangerous. In response they expect to hear, "No, ghost hunting is all harmless fun." This is not always the truth. Ghost hunter's travel into graveyards, cemeteries, and places where spirits are known to still linger. There is always the possibility that a ghost hunter will find something that they were not ready to find. In the beginning of this book, we learned that the only ghost-hunting rule is to *be ready for anything*. Expect to find entities from all ends of the spectrum from simple disembodied ghosts that cause little if any problems to heartless evil spirits that want nothing but destruction. If you are a ghost hunter long enough, you will see and experience everything. Let's just hope that you can avoid any serious dangers.

Remember that ghosts always have the upper hand on us. Do not let your guard down even for a second. Ghosts can see us when we cannot see them. Ghosts can appear where they want, when they want. Ghosts can hear conversations that we have in private. Ghosts can watch us secretly. And in some extremely rare cases, ghosts can attack us. Ghost hunters are vulnerable.

Some ghosts and spirits are territorial. They do not like it when the living invade their favorite resting places. These spirits remain in close proximity to these special places and will defend them. They may start out with some subtle hints like loud noises or equipment problems, but if their warnings are not heeded, the spirit activity may escalate to violent and dangerous activity. Always research and examine each case before jumping into the ghost hunt.

Moving Objects

Ghosts and spirits can both move objects. When ghosts move objects, the intention is not malicious. They sometimes do it to get the attention of the living, but not always. Ghosts will move objects as subtle reminders of their presence. They might also move an object, like a piece of furniture, because it makes the room look more like it did when they were alive. Ghosts may move around pieces of their favorite jewelry or common household items.

There are spirits that can pose as a ghost and move life-like objects such as dolls, stuffed animals, or figurines. Spirits do this type of object moving for the sole purpose of attempting to trick the living into believing that the object is alive or possessed. Dolls can be posed a particular way or continuously moved to different locations to give the impression that they are moving under their own control. This is never the case. Inanimate objects cannot be alive or possessed by a spirit or ghost. Spirits use these methods because it makes it much easier for the living to give recognition to earthly objects than to an invisible entity. Typically, malicious spirits will disguise themselves as the ghosts of  children claiming to be inside a doll. Again, this is because the living are much more likely to communicate with the lonely, lost ghost of a child than a spirit. The spirit plays on the feelings of human compassion to get recognition, which will give them power. The more recognition they receive from the living, the more power they get to influence the environment. Eventually, with enough recognition, the spirit can take on poltergeist-like attributes and begin moving other household objects, manipulating electrical devices, and influencing the dreams of the living.

Ghost hunters are usually called into these types of spirit cases too late. The people involved have already given the spirits too much recognition and now the situation is out of control. The first thing the ghost hunter must do is to remove the object that seems to be causing the problems. Destroy it if necessary. Order everyone involved in the case to stop giving recognition to the spirit. This means no more talking to them or taking part in any form of spirit communication. When the objects are removed and the recognition stops, it is usually only a matter of time before the power of the spirit diminishes and they look elsewhere for individuals to torment.

As a ghost hunter, it is your job to conclude whether a non-threatening ghost or a spirit with an agenda is moving the object. Typically, these cases are not hard to determine. Object moving by ghosts is usually not done for the sole purpose of getting the living's attention. The objects movement might not have much of an effect on the people involved. The locations surrounding the ghost movement often have a history of haunting activity that can be traced back to past events. Object moving by ghosts is usually not the only paranormal activity to occur at a haunted location. It's exactly the opposite in the case of a spirit moving objects.

The objects that are moved by spirits are moved for the sole purpose of attracting the living to the object. Objects are moved in a more obvious fashion and are often positioned to give the false appearance that they are alive. The location typically does not display any past evidence of a haunting. It usually does not have any other haunting characteristics until after the spirit has gained enough power from human recognition. It's important to know that both ghosts and spirits can move objects for different reasons. It is very important to be able to clearly distinguish between the two different instances.

Conducting Cemetery and Haunted House Ghost Hunts

Arrive early with your necessary ghost hunting equipment and give yourself plenty of time to set everything up. Here is a quick list of some equipment you may wish to use: a video camera, EMF detectors, 35 mm cameras loaded with brand new film and thermometers. Always remember to bring along plenty of flashlights. Don't forget to bring along some patience. Conducting a ghost hunt is a lot like fishing. You have to use patience.

Start by selecting a private room or a general location for a main base of operations. This base is where all monitoring should be done. It should not be an area where ghost activity is high. After the base has been selected, do a complete walkthrough of the general area. Check out every room, and in graveyards, walk around the tombstones in a 50-yard radius. Videotape the walkthrough if you are using video cameras. Make sure that you know the layout before you begin the ghost hunt. Get used to the location. The ghost hunt will go much better if everyone feels comfortable with the surroundings.

Use the EMF detectors to search for anything out of the ordinary. If you do pick up EMF distortions or if you feel that there is an unearthly presence nearby, take more photos. Just be aware that in cemeteries smooth glossy tombstone faces will reflect light from the flashlights or the camera flash that could create strange light patterns in the pictures. Glass objects and mirrors will reflect light inside houses.

During the initial walkthrough or at any other time during the ghost hunt, try not to unnecessarily touch or move objects. You should leave the natural environment alone. As you are doing the walkthrough in haunted houses, hang up ghost catchers in doorways, between rooms, or on staircases. If a ghost passes near the ghost catcher, they will chime alerting anyone nearby. A lightweight wind chime will suffice.

If there are objects or pieces of furniture that have been reported to move, put a chalk line or sticker on the floor next to these objects. That way, if the objects happen to move, you have a marker to judge and measure the exact distance.

Everyone participating in a ghost hunt should always know where everyone else is to avoid confusion and misinterpretations. Sometimes handheld or headset radio communicators are good devices to stay in contact with the other ghost hunting members.

° Always log every event that seems out of the ordinary, (doors that lock, electrical problems, swaying chandeliers, strange lights, etc). Videotape everything for proof.

You can attach glow-in-the-dark or reflective tape to objects to help you with the layout and to mark special locations. The tape will make it much easier to see dangerous objects in the dark. You don't need to turn off the lights inside of the haunted house to have ghosts appear unless it is vital to the appearance of that particular ghost. Even then, leave some lights on for personal safety. Always have a couple of mini spotlights ready for outside ghost hunts in case something happens and you need light fast.

Do not be afraid to experiment on ghost hunts. Ask the ghosts to appear. Put the video cameras on different settings. Try the EVP audio taping methods. Use anything that you think might have an effect on the ghosts. If nothing seems to be happening, you might try to shake things up by playing religious or music that would be familiar to the ghost.

On any ghost hunt, make sure to have packed plenty of snacks, drinks, and maybe a board game. Ghost hunts can be long and tedious. You may have to spend several weeks inside at a haunted location before you experience anything strange.

Simple Ghost Hunting Techniques

Here are a few simple ghost-hunting techniques that can be used to uncover the work of a fraud. These methods can also be used to help prove that someone is not falsely creating the haunting activity. Many of these techniques are easy to perform and the materials are cheap.

Talcum Powder: If suspicious ghost activity is centered in one room try using this experiment. After dark, spread a light layer of plain talcum powder onto the floor. Do not tell anyone outside your own group that this has been done. In the morning, check to see if anything in the room has been disturbed. Look at the layer of talcum powder on the floor and see if it is disturbed. Sometimes you'll be able to find human footprints or animal paw prints that can shed some light on the haunting activity. If the haunting continues and the powder is not disturbed, that is further evidence that points toward the paranormal. You can also put the talcum powder on window seals and near doorways.

Cotton Balls: You can use cotton balls to put in the top of door hinges between the wall and the door. Close the door with the cotton ball hidden in the doorframe. If someone should attempt to enter the room that was not supposed to, the cotton ball will fall out of place when the door opens. Cotton balls can also be placed underneath doors and in window seals or anywhere you want to detect movement.

Hidden Video Cameras: Small surveillance video cameras can be purchased at many local security stores. The cameras can be incredibly tiny, some no bigger than a button. These can be hidden in rooms with paranormal activity. The cameras can give a better insight into what is actually happening when no living person is around. Tiny surveillance cameras are becoming more affordable and some stores rent them out.

Use Chalk Marks: Put chalk marks or outlines next to objects that are moving. If the object does happen to move, you can measure the exact distance that the object has traveled. It is also important to take note of which direction the object is moving.

Watching Human Hands: If you are with a group of people inside a haunted house and start hearing strange noises, make a quick check of everyone's hands. There have been cases where individuals have been pressing a secret button to create sound effects in other parts of the house. Always keep a close eye on individuals when unexplained activity begins to occur. Make a mental note of individuals that leave or who are never present during those times.

Florescent Powders and Gels: These powders and gels are invisible to the naked eye. You can rub them on objects to find out if a living person is manipulating objects. You can conduct easy experiments like smearing the florescent gel onto a magic marker. Then, lay it next to some blank sheets of paper out in the open where ghosts can use them to communicate. Later, if there is something written on the paper, pull out the black light. The florescent material glows brightly under the black light. Anyone trying to commit a fraud by writing the message would be caught glowing handed.

Tips On Using EMF Detectors

Hold the EMF detector about two feet from your body or anyone else's body at all times. If the EMF detector is held too close to a living object, it might mistakenly read your own electromagnetic field.

Don't stand too close to other electrical equipment, (video camcorders, computers, televisions, etc.). Any electrical device can give off enough EMF to cause the EMF detectors to create false readings. Remove all electrical equipment from your body before using an EMF detector.

There are some EMF detectors that can automatically weed out manmade EMF signals from everyday household electrical appliances, but most common brand EMF detectors are very sensitive. It's import to record any parts of a room where manmade EMF signals are going to distort readings, (electrical sockets, groups of wires behind walls, alarm clocks, etc.). Remove any electrical appliances you can and make detailed notes on the rest.

Always perform background readings first. Background readings will provide neutral data to compare paranormal readings. Background readings are done by going outside of the paranormal area and recording EMF readings. Once at least three background readings are performed, record them in a notebook. Then, slowly move into the paranormal area continuing to record the EMF readings. Any changes in the EMF fields are important to note. Unexplainable variations between the paranormal area and the background area could indicate that something paranormal is occurring.

When using an EMF detector always have 35-mm cameras, video cameras, and audio recorders ready to operate. If changes in the EMF field are detected, start using the other technical equipment. Take pictures, shoot video, and turn on the audio recorders. Later, go back and review the evidence to see if the equipment recorded anything strange. Typically, orbs, weird lights, mists, and voices will be recorded in simultaneous reaction with the EMF detectors. Be aware that any audio recordings might be hard to listen to if a nearby EMF detector has a loud audio signal. Turning down the volume level is possible so that the audio signal sound doesn't distort other audio recordings.

EMF Detectors and IR Thermometers are excellent to use together. IR Thermometers are devices that let the operator instantly record the surrounding environments temperature. Used together, the IR Thermometer will show any strange drops in temperature in areas where the EMF detectors reads abnormal EMF fields. It is not recommended to use EMF detectors for extended amounts of time in temperatures below 30 degrees Fahrenheit or over 100 degrees Fahrenheit, as extreme temperatures will damage the sensitive circuits inside the equipment.

Always secure EMF detectors, and all other sensitive equipment, in protective cases for travel. EMF detectors can be wrapped in bubble wrap or surrounded by sponge cushions. It is important to keep EMF detectors from bouncing around while traveling. The better they are taken care of, the longer they will last. If an EMF detector takes too many hard knocks, the accuracy caliber will suffer.

Science and Ghost Hunting

When mainstream scientists debunk ghosts, their first statement is usually, "there is no scientific proof of the existence of ghosts." This is wrong. There is scientific proof. Science even has theories that state something must be happening beyond what we know and what we can see.

Albert Einstein (1879-1955), one of the greatest minds the world has known, taught us that energy could not be created or destroyed. It can only be changed from one form of energy into another form of energy. This means that no matter what is done, energy cannot be destroyed.

Human beings have both electrical and chemical energy in their bodies. We are organically designed to carry our electrically charged brain and nervous systems. When we die, our chemical bodies begin to break down and decompose. The organic side returns to where it came from - energy changing into a different form of energy as Einstein's law states. So what happens to the electrical energy that flows through our brain? It cannot simply disappear or fade away out of existence because that would break the laws of science. That electrical energy has to be changed into a different form of energy. No one knows exactly what waits beyond this life. What we do know, thanks to science, is that the electrical pulse energy in each human being will always exist because as a rule, "it cannot be destroyed."

Another great scientist who believed in life after death was Thomas Edison, (1847-1931). Edison was a genius ahead of his time. He invented the light bulb, phonograph, typewriter, electric motor, stock ticker, and 1,093 other patented inventions. One of the inventions that he worked on at the end of his career was a secret project, a machine that would let the living see and communicate with the souls of the dead.

Edison believed that that the soul was made up of what he referred to as, "life units." These microscopic particles, or life units, could rearrange into any form. They retained full memory and personality, and were indestructible. Edison's machine would detect these life units in the environment and allow the living to communicate with the dead. He put many years of hard work into his new creation, but sadly, he died before it was finished. Some called Edison crazy. Others thought that he was onto something bigger than the idea of the light bulb. They believed that if he would have had a little more time, we might all be living in a very different world today.

Electrical elements have been found in many ghost haunts and poltergeist cases. Using EMF detectors, ghost hunters can monitor these electrical forces. These devices can examine and record even the smallest fluctuation in the surrounding electromagnetic fields. Everything gives off some kind of electromagnetic field, even our own bodies. Electrical appliances like television sets and computers give off higher distortions than a lamp or a toaster would. When ghosts are present, there are higher levels of electromagnetic distortions. Many times the distortions are so high, they interfere with the working abilities of household electrical devices. High levels of static electricity are also detectable.

Recording temperature changes is another scientific way of detecting the presence of ghosts. Fluctuations of more than 10 degrees have been recorded in small areas of rooms with constant temperatures. It is a scientific fact that there has to be some form of energy present to alter the temperature. Temperature does not change unless something is affecting it one way or the other. In many ghost sightings, witnesses report feeling a cold spot. This could be caused by the fact that light does not seem to reflect correctly off of most ghosts, which also gives them a dark form. The light seems to be absorbed into the ghost. The theory is that ghosts absorb both light and heat energy causing the general area around that ghost to be several degrees cooler. There are also hot spots recorded, which could be just the reverse affect occurring. Instead of soaking up the light and heat, the ghost is reflecting it back, causing the area to be warmer.

These unexplainable electromagnetic fluctuations and temperature changes are scientific evidence that something is happening. Ghosts are real.

The Psychology of Grief

Death is a normal, expected part of human existence and the grief associated with it is intensely personal. Grief is a natural aid that allows deep emotional wounds time to heal. It should not be suppressed, but it is important not to let the grief become all consuming and destructive. Paranormal investigations have consistently revealed that the root of a haunting is often a massive amount of grief emanating from an earlier tragic incident. The strong feelings of sadness and regret are frequently the main source behind many ghosts.

There are five stages of grief: Denial, Bargaining, Anger, Depression, and finally, Acceptance. Each stage represents a step in the recovery process. None of the stages have an exact time frame. The healing process will vary depending on the grieving individual and the circumstances of the trauma. Because of the personal nature of grief, there is almost nothing that a living person can do to help a grieving ghost. The healing process cannot be forced. The good intentions of the living attempting to help a ghost can actually backfire and push the ghost deeper into their grief. A person, or ghost, must deal with grief on their own terms, in their own time.

When sudden, unexpected deaths occur in the forms of accidents, disasters, suicides, murderer, etc., the experience can cause devastating emotional trauma. Bereavement can be so commanding that it makes people want to disappear or separate from the reality of the world. Isolation and confusion causes the feelings of grief to snowball out of control. Emotional energies can fluctuate to dangerous levels. Ghosts feel the same emotional trauma that living individuals battle with on a daily basis. A ghost who suffered grief in their lifetime seems to separate from the reality of death. The ghost refuses to "move on." Denial is an early stage of the grief process. Grief is universal. The moods of bereavement can change rapidly, seesawing back and forth from calm reflections to paralyzing misery. A stimulation of the human senses; a smell, sound, touch, thought, or an image, can cause intense emotions to flood back to the surface. The "mood swings" of ghosts are the same as living individuals. Ghostly activity can increase when a stimulus unlocks a feeling or memory from their past life. Examples of these stimuli can include playing period music, reading a favorite poem aloud, a recognizable scent, a familiar looking visitor, etc. While many ghosts will respond to some form of familiar stimulus, there are ghosts that will not respond to any stimuli. The reasons for ghosts ignoring the stimulus could be that an unknown factor is keeping the ghost from experiencing the stimulus. Or, the ghost might be in a deep state of denial, refusing to acknowledge any evidence that they are deceased.

A grief stricken ghost must progress through the stages of grief before they will be free to "move on" to whatever else awaits them in the afterlife. Surviving grief is not as easy as "getting over it." Human emotions are so powerful that they continue to drive the soul even after death. Working to relinquish earthly attachments, while overcoming the anguish and despair associated with grief, can be the release that these tormented souls desperately need. In the end, all souls must struggle to find peace.

Questions and Answers (Q&A)

These are the answers to some of the most common questions that people have about ghosts and the paranormal.

Q: Are ghosts real?
A: A majority of ghost and haunting cases do turn out to have a logical "earthly" explanation. However, there are percentages of cases that cannot be explained in scientific or logical terms. These cases defy all sensible explanations and seem to point to the supernatural for their causes, meanings, and origins. There is reason enough from the circumstantial evidence to believe that ghosts, being defined as returning souls of the deceased, are in fact real. For additional information read the **Famous Ghost Stories**, chapter.

Q: Are ghosts good or bad?
A: They can be both. Ghosts are the souls of deceased living beings. Some people are good and some people are bad. Ghosts are no different. Ghosts are not demonic or evil by nature, but they can be considered frightening. A common misconception is that ghosts have something to do with demons. Ghosts are not demons and demons do not haunt homes. Ghosts do haunt, but that does not mean they are trying to chase everyone else way from that house. Ghosts tend to act much like they did in life; some days are better than others.

Q: Are ghosts that appear grayish or black evil or threatening?
A: No. Another common misconception is that a ghost that manifests itself in a gray or black form must be an evil spirit. This is not at all true. The color of the apparition has nothing to do with its personality. Many ghosts appear in dark forms because the light is not reflecting correctly off of them. The feeling of evil that people reported being felt around dark shaded apparitions is usually only the natural human feelings of fear. When people are afraid, their emotions control their mindset. Personal and religious beliefs also play into these misinterpreted assumptions.

Q: Can animals return as ghosts?

A: Yes. There are many homes and pet cemeteries that report the ghosts of animals haunting the grounds. Usually, the animals are common household pets. Sometimes the animals had been physically mistreated or tortured in life. The big question that manifests from this is that of whether or not animals have souls. Most research and thought has shown that it's a safe assumption to say yes animals have souls. Their souls are obviously not the same as a human soul, but nevertheless they do have a life force. There is a theory that people sometimes give their animals a soul through their love and affection. That theory is fine, but it does not appear to work in all cases. There are phantom cats and other phantom animals that had no owners or owners that mistreated them.

Q: Am I in any danger if my home is haunted?

A: It depends upon your case. A ghost haunting will not be dangerous. The ghosts are there whether living individuals are present or not. The biggest physical threat tends to happen at the time that the persons are seeing a ghost. Most people panic. Sometimes the fear is so great that the person has to run away. Typically, at this time, it is dark, and running in the dark can be dangerous. Emotionally, ghost sightings can be very traumatic for the living. People who are easily frightened should not try to handle ghost hunting. It's really up to each person's own mental state. Just because ghosts are not a violent entity, does not give license for carelessness. In some rare cases, the ghosts may actually turn out to be a poltergeist, which can cause harm to the living. Any cases involving children should also be watched for any troubling warning signs, such as strange scratches, bruises, violent behavior, and spontaneous outbursts. Always think safety first.

Q: Can a ghost follow me from place-to-place?

A: It's very rare. For the most part, ghosts are haunting a location. The haunting has nothing to do with you. A poltergeist can and do follow people from place to place. If an object is the source of the haunting, anyplace that object goes, the ghostly activity will follow. There are other exceptions like the *family apparition*, which are ghosts that are tied to a specific family.

Q: Can objects become haunted?

A: Yes. It does appear that objects can become haunted, but not possessed. There is a difference. Sometimes the haunting is from the ghost of a past owner or creator who had a strong emotional tie to the object. Other objects seem to be cursed or corrupted with some other supernatural force.

Q: Do ghosts communicate with the living?

A: Some ghosts do. Some ghosts do not or are unable to communicate. There are ghosts that frequently attempt to communicate with the living in one form or another.

It might be with a voice or it could be through banging sounds or by moving objects. Communication from ghosts is also done through writing, expressions, thoughts, and dreams. Ghosts that want to communicate will do just about anything to get noticed. Some ghosts that people encounter seem to be either unable or unwilling to communicate. They go about their own business and have little interest in the living.

Q: Are ghost sightings more common at night?
A: No. There is no certain time of day that is more frequent for ghost sightings. It's a very common misconception that ghosts will only appear at night, particularly midnight, the, *witching hour*. Ghosts can manifest at any time of the day or night. One ghost may appear only at one time of the day, while another ghost may appear randomly at all times of the day. Their appearances typically depend on the circumstances that surround the origins of each ghost. Ghost hunters sometimes forget this rule and get caught up searching for a ghost late at night. That does not do much good when the ghost hunter later discovers that the ghost they were looking for only appears at 3 P.M.

Q: What should I do if I see a ghost?
A: Don't be afraid. Typically, the only people that get hurt during a ghost sighting are those people who try to run away and end up tripping and falling. Don't let your fear cause you to do anything rash. Instead, watch the ghost. Examine what it does. Try to keep mental notes on every detail. Try to communicate. Seeing a ghost is a once in a lifetime opportunity. Take advantage of it. After the sighting has ended, be sure to write every thing down while the experience is fresh in your memory.

Q: Why do ghosts wear clothes?
A: Traditional ghosts manifest in clothing from their own time period. Sometimes ghosts will change their clothes, but most of the time, ghosts continually manifest wearing exactly the same thing. No one really knows why. Some theories maintain that the ghosts feel more comfortable in those clothes or that the clothes themselves are somehow directly connected to the haunting. For example, ghosts of dead soldiers are seen wearing their military uniforms. Phantom monks appear in their robes. The clothes seem to be what the ghosts remember from their life. There has never been a report of a ghost that has updated their dress style to keep up with the current times. There are some reports of ghostly nudists. These cases are very interesting. No clothes in life and no clothes as a ghost. As if ghosts weren't scary enough!

Q: Can dreams be mistaken for something supernatural?
A: Yes. Many people have stories that begin with them going to sleep. They say that something wakes them up, like a strange noise or flash of light. They find that they are unable to move and feel paralyzed. They notice dark, sometimes distorted figures, looming in the corners of the room. Despite being in plain viewing, they cannot

exactly make out what they are seeing. They hear strange noises and bright flashes of light that appear with no sources. Most people do not remember how the experience ends. They are dazed and confused. This experience is called a lucid dream. The dreamer never woke up in the first place. None of the experiences ever happened despite the incredible realistic visions. It's hard to tell what was real and what was a dream. Lucid dreaming is a very real, but rare occurrence. Lucid dreams typically happen in women more than men. Some stimulants that can cause lucid dreaming are stress, anxiety, and sexual problems. There are also other dream and sleep disorders that can cause similar occurrences.

Q: If Parapsychology subjects like ESP are true, why aren't people winning big at Casinos?
A: Some people do claim to win money in casinos by using ESP. The problem is, it takes tremendous practice and concentration because the casino environments are deliberately set up to confuse the players. Casinos have bright lights and flashy signs that divert players' attention. Loud noises and chattering voices make it hard for a player to clear their mind, with the rush of gambling and free alcohol to top it off. Casinos have every variable that has been shown to produce poor ESP results in laboratory settings and it's not by accident. Casinos know what they are doing.

Q: Is the invisible friend of my child really a ghost?
A: It's very unlikely. Children have incredible imaginations that can create elaborate invisible friends, which are very real to them. Some parents do not understand this and become worried that their child's invisible friend is really a ghost in disguise. It's probably not the case. However, where children are involved, there should always be a great deal of caution used. Talk to the child. Watch what they do and how they act. Be on the lookout for any troubling or violent warning signs that could be a signal of something beyond the normal realm of a playful imagination.

Q: Can anyone absolutely prove that ghosts really exist?
A: At this time, the answer is no. There is an endless supply of circumstantial evidence that points to the existence of ghosts: witness sightings, pictures, video clips, etc. All of this evidence would be sufficient in any other field, but not ghost hunting. Since the early days of ghost hunting, there have been major technological breakthroughs that give ghost hunters the capability to monitor changes in the environment when ghosts are present. Obviously something is happening. The proof will come in the future.

Q: Can a person have an abnormal electromagnetic field surrounding them making them more susceptible to paranormal events occurring around them?
A: All living creatures have electromagnetic fields surrounding them. It does appear that there are some individuals who have abnormal electromagnetic fields and

experience more paranormal activity, (flicker lights, high levels of static electricity, sudden failure of electrical appliances, etc.). There are even people who cannot pass through retail store security systems without setting them off. There are not many explanations as to why some individuals have these abnormal electromagnetic fields.

Q: Can Ghosts Attack People?
A: 99.9 percent of all ghosts are completely harmless to living individuals. Many ghosts seem unaware of the presence of the living. Most human injuries come from witnesses running away from a frightening experience. There have been reports of "ghosts" attacking people. These reports involve individuals who have been scratched, slapped, pushed, etc. However, when these "ghost attack" cases are studied, it becomes clear that almost all of the attacks are not done by a typical ghost/haunting, but instead perpetrated by poltergeist energy or another supernatural entity.

Q: Is there a Bogeyman?
A: The Bogeyman is from British Folklore and is synonymous with evil spirits and hobgoblin-like monsters. The Bogeyman is usually described as an ominous creature that scares sleeping children. To answer the question: No, there is not a monster called the Bogeyman that hides underneath beds to scare little children at night. However, there are evil spirits. Ghosts and evil spirits can do basically the same thing that the Bogeyman has a reputation for doing, scaring children. So, maybe, in a roundabout way, there are Bogeymen.

Q: Is it okay to use Ouija Boards, Magic Spells, or Séances while ghost hunting?
A: None of the above can be considered acceptable ghost hunting tools. From a scientific viewpoint, the validity of the methods involved in using each of these devices can be questioned. There's no evidence that Ouija Boards, Magic or Séances can produce consistent and accurate results. Many people also believe that evil spirits are drawn directly to these types of activities.

Q: Are ghosts more active during the "witching hour?" (Midnight to 3 a.m.)
A: There are investigators that believe the witching hour produces more paranormal activity because of the position of the moon and its magnetic effects on the earth. Results, and the amount of effects, will vary from case to case. It is known that the moon influences ocean tides, but there is no evidence that the moon's magnetic pulls influence human or supernatural behavior.

Q: Where can I get a parapsychology degree? Can I get one off of the Internet?
A: A degree in the field of parapsychology requires attending a graduate school. To get into any of the top schools to study parapsychology, you must first have a Maters Degree in a science-related field, (Math, Statistics, any of the Social or Behavioral

Sciences, Law, etc.). Contrary to what some people may believe, you cannot get a real parapsychology degree from an Internet website that is not affiliated with a college, even if that website is run by a licensed parapsychologist.

Parapsychologists are doctors. They can write medical prescriptions to calm nerves or for sleeping medications and are state board certified. The Parapsychological Association is an elected affiliate of the American Association for the Advancement of Science (AAAS). If someone is masquerading as a parapsychologist without the credentials, they are running the serious risk of criminal penalties and civil lawsuits. (To find more information on parapsychology, including journals, schools, and institutes, see the **Paranormal Organizations** chapter.)

Q: I recently purchased a house that is haunted, is there anything that I can do?
A: There is almost nothing that can be done to get rid of a ghost. There are some things that you might try, but don't expect great results. (See **Getting Rid of Ghosts** in the **Things that Ghost Hunters Should Know** chapter.) You might also want to check with a knowledgeable real estate agent or an attorney specializing in real estate cases. There are a few states that have laws against selling a "known" haunted house without informing the buyer. If you bought the home knowing that there might be ghosts, you have little recourse. Real estate laws vary from state to state. It's always good to know your legal options.

Q: Can a murdered person's ghost haunt their killer?
A: That's a hard question to answer. It's difficult to get law-abiding people to talk about a haunting. It would be even harder to get a criminal to tell you about a ghost, especially if the ghost was someone that they had killed. There is not enough information to give a valid yes or no answer, but there are a few known tales of ghosts coming back from the grave to torment and get even with their attackers. However, in many haunting cases involving a murder, the ghost will haunt the location of the murder and not the killer.

2000 cr

Parapsychology

Parapsychology is the scientific study of unusual events associated with the human experience. Parapsychology is related to the psychology field dealing specifically with the mind-body relationship. There are usually two subjects, the "human mind" and the "earthly object." Parapsychology suggests that the assumed separation between the mind and matter may be wrong. There are three main categories of parapsychology that will be discussed: ESP, Psychokinesis (PK), and the survival of the soul after bodily death. Parapsychologists believe that further research will eventually explain these anomalies in scientific terms. However, to fully understand them, the current boundaries of science may need to be expanded.

Parapsychology is NOT: Anything weird or bizarre. Parapsychology is not concerned with studies of UFO's, Bigfoot, astrology, vampires, paganism, or witchcraft. It does not involve conjuring dark forces or any other kind of voodoo magic. While parapsychology does study psychic abilities, the people who claim to be psychic are not parapsychologists. Others, who also do not qualify to be called parapsychologists, are psychic readers, fortunetellers, magicians, paranormal investigators and ghost hunters. That statement was not meant to downplay or discount the roles of any of those careers. The statement is straightforward. They are not parapsychologists and should not claim to be parapsychologists. The Parapsychological Association is an elected affiliate of the American Association for the Advancement of Science (AAAS), the largest scientific organization in the world. It is a scholarly degreed field of study.

This section will briefly touch on each topic of parapsychology. A more complete description of these topics is beyond the scope of this book.

Extrasensory Perception (ESP)

ESP, also referred to as the sixth sense, is defined as the acquisition of information by means beyond the five human senses. The information received can come from either an external event in the environment or directly from the mind of another individual in the past, present, or future.

What is ESP? Knowing what someone is going to say or do next is ESP. Knowing which card on the deck is next to be turned over is ESP. Knowing when and where something will happen is ESP. Despite the fact that ESP has been coined the sixth sense; it is not actually a sense. ESP does not require the working ability of any of the five human senses. Time, geography, intelligence, education, religious beliefs, and age also do not affect the abilities of ESP.

ESP is one of the few paranormal sensory perceptions considered to be inherent in all human beings; meaning that everyone has the capacity of experiencing some level of ESP. These levels can be raised and toned through study and continual practice.

Studies done in the controlled environments of laboratories have shown that human emotion and external environmental factors can affect ESP performance for the better and worse. Relaxed individuals who believe in the paranormal tend to have a better chance of experiencing ESP. There are some talented individuals who are born with the rare gift for exceptional ESP called super ESP.

Telepathy

Remote Feeling/Perception. Telepathy is the mind-to-mind communication between individuals. It is the theory that thoughts, feelings, ideas, and images can transcend time and space. The communications can come in several different forms: visions, dreams, mental images, and fragments of thought.

The most common form of telepathy happens spontaneously during a crisis situation. Individuals receive images and mental thoughts of danger at the exact time someone they share a close emotional tie with is in trouble. Identical twins are widely known for sensing when their twin is hurt or in trouble. Sometimes the tie is so great, that they actually share the same pain in cases of injury. A mother and her child also tend to have a more heightened sense of telepathy, leading many researchers to believe that there is a biological connection in many cases.

Prayer also falls into this category. The mind-to-mind communication still counts even if one of the minds belongs to God.

Clairvoyance

Clear Seeing. Clairvoyance is the extrasensory perception manifesting in the form of either an internal or external vision of present or future events, objects, places, and people.

The extent of clairvoyant ability ranges from the strong visual image seen by the so-called "inner or third eye," to the common sensation of a gut feeling. The highest form of clairvoyance involves viewing nonphysical planes such as spiritual worlds. This intense form of clairvoyance can either happen naturally or can be induced using various techniques. Induced clairvoyance has occurred all over the world, in every culture, throughout history. Holy men, prophets, Native American shaman, and ancient Egyptian priests are some who have used dancing rituals, long fasting periods, meditation, and in some cases, hallucinogens to achieve a higher level of induced consciousness.

The Different Types of Clairvoyance:

- Astral Clairvoyance: The viewing of astral planes and their inhabitants: Angels, ghosts, and other supernatural entities.
- Dream Clairvoyance: Dreaming of an event simultaneously as it happens.
- Medical Clairvoyance: The ability to read a person's aura to diagnose illness or disease inside the human body. The most famous clairvoyant in this field was Edgar Cayce, who continuously correctly diagnosed illnesses from hundreds of miles away. He also provided the remedies for each illness.
- Spiritual Clairvoyance: The ability to see into the higher planes, such as the angelic plane, to receive spiritual information and guidance.
- Traveling Clairvoyance: The most common of the clairvoyant abilities. The ability to see objects, places, and people from far distances transcending time and space.
- X-Ray Clairvoyance: Involves the ability to see inside solid objects such as boxes, rooms, and sealed envelopes.

Precognition

Pre-Knowing. With precognition, or *pre-knowing*, direct information about a future event is obtained through extraordinary means. Precognition happens spontaneously in the forms of waking visions, auditory hallucinations, and flashes of thought into the mind. It can also be induced through trances and channeling. This parapsychology subject is the most frequently reported.

Precognition typically happens within a period of 48 hours before the event happens. It is very rare for a precognition experience to involve far off future events. The events usually have a negative nature, including sudden illnesses, deaths, accidents, and natural disasters. A high percentage of reported precognition cases involve family members, close friends, or loved ones. This causes extremely powerful feelings of guilt in those who have experienced precognition. It can be frustrating and disappointing to see a terrible event happen beforehand and not be able to stop it or save any lives. Most people with this extra sense feel that it was given to them to help change the world for the better.

Precognition should not be confused with a premonition. Precognition involves specific knowledge of a future event. A premonition is a feeling that something is about to happen.

Psychokinesis (PK)

Mind movement, or psychokinesis (PK), is the apparent ability to influence the environment by intention alone. Psychokinesis is broken down into two separate groups. The first group, micro-PK, is when the effects studied are on a very small scale. They are usually only detectable by statistical analysis in a scientific laboratory. The second group is macro-PK. This is where the effects can be seen or witnessed by the naked human eye, (poltergeist activity, moving objects).

Psychokinesis can occur spontaneously or be created deliberately, which indicates to researchers that it is both a conscious and unconscious phenomena. It does not appear, from the initial research, that psychokinesis is connected to any physical process of the brain. Nor does it seem to be subject to any of the mechanical laws of physics or gravity. It has been a difficult subject to research and study because psychokinesis seems to work completely outside the known laws of science. Psychokinesis is a nonphysical force of mind over matter. Exactly how it works still remains a scientific enigma.

Psychokinesis in ghost hunting occurs most commonly in poltergeist cases with the movement of objects, levitation, apports (manifestation or appearance of a real object) and asports (teleportation or disappearance of a real object), rapping sounds, table tipping, and musical instruments that, seemingly, play on their own. Psychokinesis can also occur in haunting cases, but not quite to the high degree of poltergeists. In haunting cases, apparitions seem to control the unexplainable phenomena, such as doors that open and close, lights turning off and on, unexplained footsteps and unexplained ghostly sounds, etc.

Out-of-Body Experience (OBE)

OBE is a phenomenon in which a person feels separated or projected from their body. Their soul is free to travel to other earthly locations or spiritual destinations. These people are not dead, dying, or even sick. OBE occurs when the body is in a deep dream or trance-like state of relaxation.

It has been a belief held by many cultures throughout history that the mind and body are two separate entities; the body being no more than a vehicle or container for the soul. At times, it seems that somehow the soul can detach itself from the body while the body is still living. The soul is then free to consciously travel without the physical means of the body.

This phenomenon has been recorded throughout history and has been preformed by holy men, shaman, yogis, and Christian Saints to achieve more spiritual enlightenment.

Near Death Experience (NDE)

NDE is a phenomenon in which a person clinically dies, or comes very close to death, only to be revived and able to recall, in great detail, stories of spiritual worlds and other supernatural events. Individuals typically report feeling that they were floating outside of their body. Sometimes they can watch the scene from above their physical bodies, seeing and hearing everything that happens. Other people leave this realm during a near death experience and travel to a spiritual place. There are reports of near death patients traveling down long pathways and tunnels of light seeing deceased friends and relatives.

Religious beliefs and near death experiences have no apparent connection. Many different people from all races, economic status, and religious backgrounds report basically the same stories. Even individuals who did not believe in a life after death have reported experiencing things that they could not understand.

Because the elements of near death experiences are so common, (tunnels of light, seeing relatives, etc.), scientific researchers want to believe that these near death visions are only hallucinations caused by neurons firing off in the brain or by a final release of endorphins. However, with more investigation, they would realize that not all the near death cases are alike. There are cases of patients clinically dead for long enough time periods that no chemical or electrical pulses were left in their body. There are also the rarely reported near death cases of those few unlucky individuals that do not see the tunnels of light or loved ones. Instead they go to a dark place, filled with hatred, surrounded by what they called a powerful evil feeling that hovers around them. Many believe this to be a state of Hell. After near death experiences, people tend to lose their fear of dying and focus on living a better life.

Lucid Dreaming

Dreams are covered in Parapsychology because some dreams have elements of the paranormal intertwined in them. There are dreams that involve clairvoyance, precognition, and telepathy, (when two people share the same dream). Past life experiences may also project through a dream into the conscious memory.

Lucid dreaming is a common player in supernatural investigations. A person having a lucid dream is not aware of the fact that they are dreaming. Their dream is so real and lifelike that it becomes impossible to determine what was real and what was a dream. The lucid dreamer becomes confused and disoriented.

Lucid dream characteristics include feeling paralyzed, flying, levitating, intense emotions, seeing fantastic colors and bright images, and seeing dark figures and strange monstrous faces. Lucid dreaming can be a traumatic experience because the dreamer is unaware that all of these things are just a dream. Most lucid dreams begin with the dreamer going to sleep. They remember waking up and not being able to move, feeling paralyzed. They see flashing colors and dark figures in the room. They struggle inside their minds to escape this torturous experience, but they cannot. The problem is that they are not awake. This is the lucid dream state and they are in a period of what is called False Awakening. They did not wake up as they thought. They only woke up inside the dream.

It is thought that everyone has at least one lucid dream in his or her lifetime. Theories for lucid dreams include personal or job related stress, recurring nightmares, and sexual problems.

Dowsing

Dowsing is a method of locating people, animals, objects, and substances by using a forked rod, a bent pair of wires, or a pendulum. Individuals using dowsing search for sources of underground water, oil, minerals, electric cables, and water pipes with a fair accuracy of success. Occasionally, dowsers will search suspected burial sites for the bodies of murder victims.

The theories behind dowsing vary. The popular theory is that there is an electro-magnetic field surrounding everything. The dowsing tool acts like an antenna picking up the sensitive fields otherwise unfelt by people. The dowsing tool will move or twitch when the electro-magnetic fields of new objects cross under them. Sources like flowing streams of underground water produce a larger, more powerful electro-magnetic field and are therefore easier to detect. Dowsing skills have also been said to be part of a person's untapped psychic ability.

Reincarnation

Reincarnation is the belief that the soul can be reborn into a new body after death. Islam, Hinduism, Buddhism, and Judaism all have beliefs about some form of reincarnation. Christianity is the only major religion that tends to reject the belief in reincarnation.

While reincarnation has not been proven absolutely, there are some strong cases that seem to point to the fact that reincarnation does occur. Children as young as three years old have been able to give entire detailed histories of their past lives. The information is so accurate that it would be almost impossible for it not to be true. Cases of individuals under hypnosis have also uncovered several past lives.

Channeling

Channeling is a form of spirit communication where an unseen entity possesses a medium in a controlled environment to impart guidance, wisdom, or future events. The channeled entity could be a deceased human being, an angel, demon, elemental, or other higher plain spirit.

Communication can occur as automatic speech or writings. Automatic speech and writing both happen when the medium is under an altered state of consciousness induced by the entity possession. The medium speaks or writes on behalf of the possessing entity. They might also receive visions and hear voices.

Channeling abilities can occur spontaneously or they can be induced by the medium. In spontaneous cases, the medium has absolutely no control over what is happening. Most mediums exhibit this ability at a very early age. Only an uncommon few will begin to exhibit these abilities in adult life without some extraordinary life experience triggering it.

PSI

Psi is a general term, introduced by Thouless and Wiesner in 1948. It refers to the factors responsible for a variety of paranormal phenomena, free from the cultural and personal assumptions of the paranormal. Psi is the "unknown factor." A psi experience has essentially two components: an event that is thought to involve psi, and a person who experiences it. Research in parapsychology concentrates on the characteristics of the person who experiences psi, the event itself, or a combination of the two.

Psi is the twenty-third letter of the Greek alphabet.

Training PSI:

There are personal, biological, and environmental factors that affect the ability of psi subjects, (ESP and Psychokinesis), both for the positive and negative. The best mental strategy for good results seems to be an attitude of "passive striving." Keep a clear idea of what you are attempting to do, but don't try to make it happen. Do not force your mind to do something. Forcing will only lead to frustration. Anxiety, negative moods, and boredom have been shown to decrease success rates. A state of physical relaxation can help achieve more positive results. Psi performances also improve with positive moods and a friendly atmosphere and environment. The mere belief in success is also important for achieving good results.

PSI Hitting and Missing:

Hitting and Missing are the terms used to characterize the responses on laboratory psi guessing tests. A correct answer is a psi hit and an incorrect answer is a psi miss.

Besides the environmental factors that may come into play during these tests, the sheep/goat effect also alters the hit/miss outcome. The terms were coined to differentiate between someone that believes in psi subjects, (a sheep), and someone that does not believe in psi subjects, (a goat). Not surprisingly, sheep usually have better results on psi tests. Nonbelievers, or the goats, tend to miss through avoidance.

An unusual amount of psi missing is also evidence for psi. A target can only be successfully and consistently missed when the test subject "knows" what that target is. In other words, statistically, there is a limit to how many misses are coincidental. They could be missing the target on a subconscious level.

The Misconceptions and Fears of Parapsychology

There are a few main reasons why the science of parapsychology remains controversial even though it has produced substantial, persuasive, and scientific results in controlled laboratories.

The role of the popular media and public tend to confuse parapsychology with unscientific beliefs and incredible stories of the paranormal. This confusion and misinterpretation have led many real scientists to instantly dismiss the entire parapsychology field without first looking at any of the evidence.

Another serious problem is that the mainstream media rarely publishes real parapsychology results. The scientific journals that do publish information on parapsychology have a low circulation rate.

Finally, the biggest problem is that most people carry the basic fear that psi might be true. There are entire lists of reasons why people fear psi subjects:

- Psi must be associated with evil forces, black magic, and witchcraft.
- Anyone who believes in psi subjects is crazy.
- If you have a psi experience, then you must be crazy.
- Thinking about psi subjects will lead to mental illness.
- Psi suggests the loss of normal boundaries.
- If ESP exists, people will be able to read my mind all the time.
- The belief in psi subjects leads to a medieval, superstitious mentality.

- Psi experiences will effect my other normal human developments.
- If psi is real then all of my religious beliefs must be wrong.

None of the above statements are true.

Responses to Common Parapsychology Criticism

Constructive criticism is an essential part of any science. Strong skepticism about parapsychology is expected. However, most of the criticisms of parapsychology are neither constructive nor scientific. A majority of the criticisms are instead based on personal prejudices and misinformation.

One of the most popular criticisms is that psi subjects violate the very principles of science and it is, therefore, impossible. It is not that psi subjects violate the principles of science. It is that current understanding of certain scientific principles are not advanced enough to comprehend these anomalies. Just in the past few years, science has made great leaps forward in the fields of technology, biology, and medicine, which have forced scientists to change and redefine the ever-expanding boundaries of science. Much of what the world knows to be possible today was thought to be impossible only twenty years ago. It is not unlike the belief that the world was flat. Until proven wrong, it was considered the standard. A great paradigm shift must occur in order for mainstream science to accept psi as a whole.

The other big criticism of parapsychology is that it does not have a repeatable experiment. There is a fundamental problem expecting parapsychology to have a repeatable experiment. When science mentions a "repeatable experiment" they mean something like a simple application that can be duplicated in a chemistry or physics class. When variable (A) and variable (B) are combined, the outcome or solution (C), will always be the same no matter who combines the variables. While this procedure will work in some sciences, it is inappropriate to hold the social and behavioral sciences to the same standards because it is impossible to recreate the same variables consistently in each experiment. Biological, personal, and environmental variables will affect each human being differently causing the human variable to constantly be altered in each experiment. Because of that, the results in each experiment will always be different.

Things That Go Bump

Apparitions

An apparition is the supernatural manifestation of the soul of a deceased person or animal. Typically referred to as ghosts, apparitions are visually experienced. Throughout history, humans have been plagued with ghosts and haunted houses. Ancient Rome is one of the first places in history were documentation has been discovered about an alleged haunted house. It was revealed in a letter written by Roman author Pliny the Young (A.D. 62-113), to a Roman patron Lucias Sura, in which Pliny describes owning a villa in Athens that no one will rent because of a ghost that haunts it. The letter continues on detailing the events of the haunting, which include loud noises in the middle of the night that grow louder and louder, and a phantom apparition of a man appearing in filth and misery. Around the same time period, the Greek biographer Plutarch (A.D. 46-120), wrote in Life if Cimon that the ghost of a murdered man was haunting the baths at Chaeronea.

Despite research efforts, very little is known about apparitions. For many paranormal investigators, ghosts are the most compelling part of the paranormal field. One thing that is known about apparitions is that no two ghosts are exactly alike. They are as complex and diverse as each living person. Every apparition will have a specific cause, origin, and meaning. It is up to the ghost hunter to analyze the facts of each case and develop solid conclusions. To help the ghost hunter acquire a better feel for the kind of apparition they are dealing with, apparition categories have been created. You will find that most apparitions will fit into at least one of these categories or share characteristics with a couple different categories.

Atmospheric Apparition:

Atmospheric apparitions are also referred to as residual haunts. This type of ghost sighting is not actually believed to be a real ghost, but is, instead, a visual "imprint" that got left behind in the environment from a past event. These events typically include, but are not limited to, violent and tragic events. Eyewitness reports see the continuous replaying of past events exactly as they happened in life. The ghostly scenes are played and replayed with both picture and sound. A particularly strange aspect of atmospheric apparitions is that the visual picture fades down over time. As the years pass the ghosts are reported to become more and more transparent until there is no picture left at all. Over time, the sound too eventually fades away.

The most popular theory for atmospheric apparitions is represented in the field of quantum physics. Light particles become suspended in the atmosphere where they remain dormant in the environment until an outside variable stimulates them. Once stimulated, the light particles vibrate in the atmosphere causing any nearby witnesses to see and experience what is basically a holographic projection of the past event. There are certain conditions needed for this phenomenon to occur that supports the particle imprint theory. The haunted location must be indoors or where weather conditions cannot interfere. These apparitions can only be seen from a particular angle and at the proper distance. This means that ten people may be in the same room, but only a few of them will be able to experience the haunting depending on where they are standing in relationship to the vibrating light particles.

Historical Apparitions:

Historical apparitions are one step up from the atmospheric category. They typically haunt older homes and appear in solid forms. These ghosts are always dressed in period clothing. They do not speak, communicate, or acknowledge the presence of the living, but simply go about their everyday routines. They can be seen in more than one location, which makes them slightly different from the atmospheric apparitions.

Recurring Apparitions:

Recurring apparitions are ghosts that appear in regular cycles over a period of time, usually once annually. This is a very popular type of ghost sighting. The date of manifestation usually takes place on an anniversary date, or a day of special importance to the ghost. These apparitions can include both the ghosts of people and animals. Reports of recurring ghosts include individuals who have committed suicide, murder victims, and entire phantom armies marching across battlefields.

Modern Apparitions:

Modern ghosts are the manifestations of present-day ghosts. Not all ghosts are two hundred-year-old dead people. Modern apparitions are relatively new ghosts, which look and sound like modern people, dressing in modern fashions, having facial hair and hairstyles equivalent to the times they lived, etc. These ghosts will have the same characteristics as older haunts, (strange noises, odd odors, cold spots, etc.). Of course, as decades of time pass by the haunting will become more traditional and the apparitions will look dated. The modern styles will continue to change, but the apparitions will not.

Crisis or Death Bed Apparitions:

These apparitions appear to family members and close friends, just before, or soon after their death. They are very common ghost sightings, but almost never occur more than four days after death. For obvious reasons, crisis apparitions are most popular during periods of war. Wartime can create hundreds of crisis apparition cases, all reporting the appearance of dying or dead service men thousands of miles away. The crisis ghost seems to be appearing one last time to fulfill a promise, say a final goodbye, express eternal love, or to help ease the sadness of death for the living left behind.

Family Apparitions:

These ghosts attach themselves to a particular family, thus the name, family apparitions. They will haunt members of a particular family throughout each generation until the family line comes to an end. These ghosts can include the ghosts of deceased family members and phantom animals. The appearance of these ghosts usually signals that someone within the family is about to die or that something tragic is about to occur. Usually, there are no prior health problems in the family until the phantom manifests. Then, family members suddenly fall ill and die or become the victims of an untimely death. Family apparitions are considered to be death omen spirits and are the hardest ghost to get rid of. All charms, spells, blessings, and exorcisms fail. That might be because these apparitions are not actually causing the deaths, but only foretelling them in an eerie manner. The only escape known for this haunting is the end of the family line.

Haunted Objects and Object Apparitions:

Haunted objects can also be referred to as cursed. This paranormal phenomenon is one of the strangest and most puzzling enigmas of all the haunting categories. Most haunts have a ghost at the center of the paranormal activity. When dealing with haunted objects, one must question how these objects became haunted. Inanimate objects were never alive and are void of a soul. Some haunted objects are spirit associated, meaning that the ghost of a past owner is now haunting the object.

Other objects leave no clue to their haunting. In the presence of haunted objects, witnesses report all types of strange occurrences such as, bizarre sounds and lights coming from the rooms where the objects are stored, the objects move when no one is touching them, and dark apparitions are sometimes seen near the objects. Haunted objects can include almost any household or manmade possession. Some of the more common haunted objects are jewelry, collectibles, wall clocks, and furniture.

There are also object apparitions. Object apparitions are the ghostly manifestation of household or manmade objects. Haunting witnesses has seen phantom swords, books, candlesticks, and lanterns.

Modes of Transportation:

Transportation apparitions are the manifestations of non-living vehicles, such as cars, trucks, buses, bicycles, carriages, trains, airplanes, and ships. They are almost always associated with violent and tragic accidents that resulted in death. The emotional imprints left behind in these kinds of horrible events are so strong that even pieces of the wreckage can become haunted or cursed. These vehicles are seen traveling back over their last routes in the reenactments of their final moments. Phantom vehicles can be dangerous apparitions because most people who see them are usually traveling in their own vehicle. Drivers can panic and may swerve to miss a collision with a phantom vehicle only to end up going off the road and crashing.

Photographic Apparitions:

Photographic apparitions are ghosts that are not seen visually, but can be photographed. Most people are completely unaware that they have even taken a photograph of a ghost until the film is developed. The ghosts appearing in photographs may appear in slightly transparent, grayish forms wearing period clothing, or more commonly, as bright white patches of concentrated energy. Some paranormal investigators believe that a ghost can also cause blurred areas and unexplained smears to appear on a photograph. This phenomenon has taken a new twist over the past couple decades with the revolution of the personal video camcorder. Apparitions, orbs, mists, and strange unexplainable light formations have been recorded accidentally by regular, everyday people who were not trying to document the paranormal and by experienced ghost hunters who were trying to capture ghosts on video.

Out-Of-Body Apparitions:

The strange sightings of out-of-body apparitions occur when witnesses report seeing the ghost of someone who is still alive and could not have been nearby at the time of the sighting. These apparitions appear in very much the same form as a regular ghost. They can be solid or transparent, acting similar to the real person. The person whose ghost was seen does not have to be dying or even sick. They can be perfectly healthy individuals. Some people say they remember everything about their out-of-body experience and give details that can be verified by witnesses. There are also a few who claim that they can induce this out-of-body experience at will, a kind of spirit jumping. Because this apparition can manifest to witnesses that may not know the individual, this sighting may be mistaken for a traditional ghost.

Natural and Fraudulent Apparitions:

A majority of all ghost reports will end up being false. This simply means that there is a logical and natural explanation for the occurrences being mistaken for something paranormal. It is the job of the ghost hunter to find and eliminate all rational explanations. Once the normal possibilities have been ruled out, the ghost hunter can then begin to investigate for more supernatural answers.

Other explanations for ghost sightings may include fraudulent reports or psychotic disorders. Individuals fake a ghost sighting for any number of reasons. Perhaps they are trying to have some fun and see if they can trick you. Or, this may be their way of getting attention. It could be a publicity stunt. It could even be a case of schizophrenia or other mental illness, which can cause delusional hallucinations.

It is important for ghost hunters to keep in mind that there are people in this world with the technology and know-how to produce a believable, fake ghost sighting. There have been fraud cases uncovered where homeowners have wired their entire house to produce fake poltergeist activities in any room, from basement to attic, on command. If the ghost hunter completes a thorough examination for logical explana-tions, a fraudulent haunting should be easy to discover. A seasoned ghost hunter with a couple dozen cases under their belt will learn to develop a second nature for uncovering frauds.

Other Paranormal Explanations:

There is a huge list of natural explanations that can produce false apparitions and haunting conditions. However, after all natural explanations have been ruled out, there are still some scientific theories, bordering on the edge of the paranormal, that must be addressed. While for some people these explanations may be as hard to believe as the existence of ghosts, they do have a foundation in actual science. Credible scientists trying to explain paranormal occurrences have put forth theories such as time-slips and psychic echoes. Time-slips are moments where the past and present collide at one point. Anyone near the time-slip will be able to see into the past. The witnesses do not realize that this is a time-slip and, instead, believe that everything they are experiencing is part of a ghostly manifestation.

Psychic echoes are sounds from the past that have been recorded onto elements in the environment like large stones and buildings. The stored up psychic echoes are triggered at random times and play back like an old record player. While these explanations are just as unproven as the existence of ghosts, they are theories that still need to be examined in every paranormal case.

Aura

An aura is believed to be a field of energy that surrounds all living creatures, (plants, animals, and human beings). For the most part, auras cannot be seen by normal human vision. They are invisible except to a few alleged clairvoyants. Clairvoyants claim that auras are multicolored mists radiating from each living creature that fade off into space as they go further away from the person. Auras consist of rays, sparks, and light streams that intermix within the brilliant colors.

Researchers believe that the magnetic fields of living creatures produce auras. It has been thought that auras may also be some kind of energy light that vibrates at frequencies beyond the normal range of human vision. The color of the aura is said to reflect health, state of mind, and spiritual development.

Banshee

Many people mistakenly confuse the banshee with a witch. A banshee is not a witch and has nothing to do with the pagan religion of Wicca. Banshees are the female omen spirits of Scotland and Ireland. They appear to families to warn off an impending violent and untimely death.

Banshees rise up from the evening fog to sing and cry mournfully into the moonlight. Their crying is not a wail, but a tormented weeping that signals imminent doom. The banshee is supposedly the spirit of a woman who had died prematurely during childbirth. Banshees walk the earth attaching their tormented souls to death's suffering and are doomed to never have a moment of peace.

Banshees are rarely seen, but rare sightings portray them as beautiful women with long flowing hair, wearing a dark cloak over top of a green dress. Their eyes shine fiery red. Sometimes the banshees wear black veils to cover their faces. Banshees have been seen flying across the sky at night and haunting hillsides overlooking graveyards.

Stories of the banshee in America began in the south at the beginning of the Revolutionary War. The Tar River near Tarboro, North Carolina, is reported to be home to one of the few American banshees. In the month of August, when the moon is new, the river banshee can be heard crying for a patriot that was drowned there by British soldiers.

Other names for the Banshee include the *Bean-Nighe* and *Bean Si*.

Battlefield Ghosts

Battlefield ghosts are the most common apparitions. A large majority of the ghosts walking the earth are the direct result of a military conflict. There are battlefield ghosts in and around almost every battlefield in the world, from ancient Roman wars to World War II battles.

Only combat veterans can truly understand the emotional stress and trauma that is produced from war. War can drive a normal person into the dark realms of insanity. The hell of battle can create horrible images inside the soldier's mind that will never be forgotten. The extreme violence, fear, and suffering emanating from thousands of fighting soldiers is the equivalent of a psychic atomic bomb going off. The psi energy derived from warfare literally scars the earth and all of the nearby objects creating ghosts that may last for centuries.

Sounds are the most common characteristic of battlefield haunts, (soldier's yelling out orders, screaming in pain, the noises of bombs exploding and weapons firing, airplanes crashing, etc). Phantom apparitions are a rare characteristic, but they do appear. Ghosts can be seen, dressed in their military uniforms, fighting their way across the battlefield, sometimes wounded and wrapped in bloody bandages. Most battlefield ghost sightings are residual, meaning that the ghosts seem to be reenacting a real moment from the battle. There are times, however, when a battlefield ghost will make contact with living observers by telling them to run away or by making eye contact in an expressive manner.

Floating battlefields are probably the oddest form of battlefield apparitions. Witnesses have reported seeing glimpses of an entire battle scene hovering high above the ground. All of the soldiers, vehicles, and warfare equipment from the real battle can be seen in this type of phantom reenactment. The only detail that separates this apparition from a normal haunting is that the ghostly scene occurs a considerable distance above the ground. The distance can vary dramatically, from a couple yards to 50 or even 100 feet off the ground.

ground soldiers are not the only ghosts haunting battlefields. There are also numerous phantom aircrafts and phantom pilots. Aviation ghosts can be seen walking down old runways or appearing inside hanger photographs. Phantom bomber aircrafts and fighter planes from WWII still race over the fields where they crashed, killing their crew. The distinctive sounds of the airplane propeller and machine gun sprays can be heard by ducking witnesses on the ground. Witnesses have seen the reenactments of damaged phantom airplanes going down into open fields and behind hillsides. The impact sounds are so realistic that the witnesses, thinking that a real plane has just crashed, hurry and call police and fireman to help. Law enforcement agencies in the areas of the Battle of Britain, a World War II air war, have become so familiar with these false reports that they know from the descriptions if witnesses have actually seen the crash of a phantom aircraft.

The most common battlefield ghosts in the United States are from the Civil War (1861-65). Gettysburg and Antietam are two of the most haunted cities in the world. The ghosts now haunting those locations are a direct result of devastating Civil War battles. The sudden, violent deaths of war leave behind impressions of the lives that were lost.

Bilocation (Also See: *Double*.)

Bi-location is the appearance of the same individual in two completely different and sometimes very distant locations at the same time. The Bi-location phenomenon happens both spontaneously and voluntarily by inducing a trance-like state to produce a double that can travel to another location. The double is a false version of the real self. It acts differently, more mechanical. It usually does not speak or acknowledge the presence of others.

There are numerous Christian saints that became famous for their acts of Bi-location. In 1774, the saint Alphonsus Maria De' Ligouri was seen at the bedside of the dying Pope Clement XIV. However, at the time, De' Ligouri was confined to a jail cell four days travel from the Pope.

Crossroads

The term *crossroads* literally describes the spot where the paths of two different roads intersect. Crossroads are associated with cultural superstitions and magical influences. All sorts of supernatural forces including fairies, witches, trolls, ghosts and demons are alleged to manifest at the less traveled crossroads to conduct private activities. Haunted crossroads have long been suspected for the strange disappearance of travelers. Ghostly riders, dark apparitions, and ominous creatures have all been seen at lonely crossroads just after sunset. Legends from the Deep

South say that crossroads are places where deals with the Devil can be made, or where contests can be preformed to obtain the rights to a particular soul.

One old legend tells that the lost souls of suicide victims remain trapped at the crossroads until they are forgiven and set free. On the night of All Hallows Eve, Halloween October 31st, the souls of the dead will appear and can be conjured at the crossroads. Once the spirit of the crossroads has been called, it must answer three questions correctly.

The most famous crossroads legend comes from the Deep South delta town of Greenwood, Mississippi, where a musician named Robert Johnson traveled to a secret crossroads and made a deal with a man dressed in black so that he could learn the play the blues. After the visit to the crossroads, Robert went from not being able to play the guitar, to being one of the most influential blues musicians in history.

(Also See: *Ley Lines and Power Points*.)

Double (Sometimes referred to as *Doppelganger*.)

A double is the mirror-image apparition of a living person that appears in a distant location. Doubles are an exact false replica. They are believed to be a projection of the astral body or soul. In some beliefs, the sighting of a double is considered a death omen for the person seeing the double. In some extremely rare cases, the person sees their own double, meaning that they are about to die.

Not all appearances of a double signal a death omen. A California resident tells a strange story from her youth. She was sitting alone in her room early one Saturday morning playing with her dolls. She glanced up and was startled to see her mother standing next to her bed. She hadn't see or heard her mother enter the room. Her mother seemed to be acting strange and wasn't saying anything, but this didn't scare the little girl because the figure looked exactly like her mother. The figure slowly turned around and started to walk toward the doorway. Instead of walking out of the door, the figure passed directly through the wall. The shocked girl dropped her dolls and jumped up. When she gained enough strength, the girl ran to her mother's bedroom and found her sound asleep. It's been over two decades since this occurred. Both the mother and daughter are still alive and joke about the incident.

Earth Lights (Sometimes referred to as *Ghost* and *Spook Lights*.)

Earth Lights are luminous phenomena typically shaped in ball form or irregular patches of light appearing randomly and defying explanation. The size and color of the mysterious lights vary.

While not much is known about Earth Lights, researchers at the Ghost Research Society have identified some common characteristics:

1. They appear in remote areas.
2. They are elusive and can only be seen from the correct distance and proper angle.
3. They seem to react to both lights and noise, darting, weaving, and disappearing.
4. Gaseous materials sometimes accompany them.
5. Observers reportedly hear buzzing or humming sounds.

There are literally hundreds of active Earth Light locations in the United States and thousands across the world. Credible scientists have proposed countless theories as to the origin of the lights and their meaning. One popular theory is that seismic stresses build up beneath the earth's crust creating masses of ionized gas or plasma. There is evidence to support the seismic theory. Some of the most active Earth Light spots are in direct contact to fault lines and studies have shown that the lights are more active just before earthquakes when the stresses are at maximum levels.

There is also good evidence that some ancient cultures where aware of the Earth Lights and erected temples and megaliths in the places where the lights appeared. Not surprisingly, there are always a high number of UFO sightings at these locations. The Earth Lights are probably mistaken for UFO's as they glide over the night sky. These Earth Lights locations also seem to have a high number of haunting and poltergeist reports. Whether or not the earth energies that create the strange lights have anything to do with the paranormal remains in debate.

Ectoplasm

Ectoplasm comes from two Greek words, *ektos* and *plasma*, meaning exteriorized substance. Ectoplasm comes in two different forms. The first, and most common form, is a thick residue, usually appearing as a milky white substance. The second form is a vaporous gas. Both have an intense ozone smell. Spirits supposedly materialize as ectoplasm through the help of a medium or psychic.

Ectoplasm became popular back in the early 1900's when fraudulent mediums used it as a trick in staged séances. The fake ectoplasm, made from a mixture of soap, gelatin, and egg whites, would mysteriously appear and grow from the medium's faces, arms, and other body parts.

There are several strange characteristics associated with ectoplasm. Ectoplasm is warm to the touch. It has a wax-like composition with weight and mass. A sometimes-gelatinous, rubbery substance; it disappears suddenly when exposed to bright light. The vaporous ectoplasm is light, resembling clouds of smoke. Probably the most amazing characteristic is that ectoplasm is able to pass straight through objects without leaving a trace behind. Witnesses to the phenomena report that ectoplasm seems to take on a consciousness of its own, moving like the tentacle of an octopus.

Energy Vortexes

Vortexes are invisible locations on the earth emitting natural electrical and magnetic energy sources. These energy forces flow in and out of the earth like whirlwind tornados. Paranormal investigators study vortexes because paranormal activity is often very high in these locations. Vortexes affect the environment, animals, people, and machines. Animals can act wild or afraid. People see strange lights and experience paranormal events. Mystical healings can occur. The earth can turn color and rocks can magnetize. Compasses go out of whack and sensitive electrical equipment fails.

The unique energy from vortexes cannot be seen, smelled, or tasted. Individuals who interact with a vortex can feel the energy flow through their bodies. The energies can be electric, magnetic, or both (electromagnetic). These energies flow into and out of the earth. Each location will have different effects depending on the amount of energy at the location.

Energy vortexes come in varying sizes. Most of the vortexes associated with ghosts and small paranormal events are small and concentrated in a specific location. The large vortexes like Cathedral Rock, Boyton Canyon, and Sedona cover several square miles and have much more power. Paranormal investigators will mostly focus on the smaller vortexes. Vortexes can occur anywhere, inside caves, in riverbeds, within a house, or on the grounds of a cemetery.

Vortexes do not necessarily create paranormal activity. The vortexes energy enhances psychic abilities allowing people to experience the paranormal activity that is already occurring in that area. The vortex energies also enhance the paranormal forces causing them to happen more frequently.

When scientists examined many of these vortexes, they discovered that the vortexes were geophysical anomalies. Scientists acknowledge that locations with a vortex have unexplained electromagnetic fields, large amounts of charged ion particles flowing in the air, and cause biochemical reactions within living organisms. Scientists also discovered that all of these vortex anomalies increase days before drastic geological changes like earthquakes and volcanic eruptions. The tremendous tension and friction underneath the earth's crust drives the energies upward from deep inside the earth. The pressure builds up until the energies are pushed out of the earth. As the energies flow, rates increase. So does the paranormal activity.

When people come into contact with vortexes, they can feel the energy interacting with their own electromagnetic fields. The energy interaction is believed to be a catalyst in healing effects and in many other paranormal events that witnesses report experiencing. Scientists have established that certain biochemical reactions occur in living creatures as a result of coming into contact with energy vortexes. Every person will react differently at each vortex because everyone has a different electromagnetic field.

Ancient civilizations could feel the vortex energies and built sacred temples and holy shrines on the locations to amplify these energies. It was believed by early cultures that these areas were divine transmitters where individuals could receive spiritual wisdom and strength. Every ancient culture in the world experienced and interacted with vortex energies. Early Europeans erected stone megaliths on them. The great Aztec culture built pyramid temples on them. The Chinese called the energy Yin and Yang. Australian Aborigines named the energy flows Spirit Lines. Native Americans call them Spirit Paths.

Exorcism

Exorcism is a religious rite preformed by a holy man for the purpose of expelling an evil spirit or demon. There are basically two types of exorcism. The first is a bodily exorcism where a religious ceremony is preformed to cast out any evil spirits or demons from the body of a possessed person. The exorcism can last for days, months, or years depending on the grip that invading entity holds on its unwilling host. Bodily possession is considered to be an evil or demonic act in most

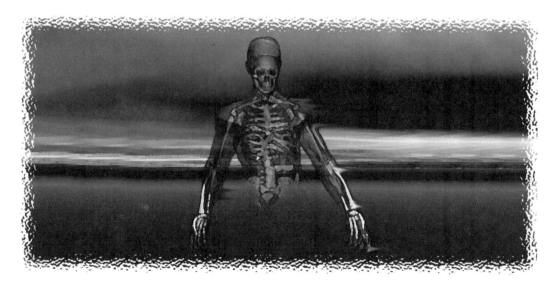

cultures and religions.

The rite of exorcism performed by the Roman Catholic Church is called the Rituale Romanum. The Catholic exorcist must stand firm in their religious conviction and believe strongly in the power of Jesus Christ. To the Church, the exorcism itself is considered a battle between God and the devil where the host and exorcist's souls are both up for grabs. The possessed individual may shout out the past sins of the exorcist or try to shake their faith by twisting words, confusing the tired exorcist. The slightest doubt of faith or hesitation will be destructive to the success of the exorcism. The exorcist must be ready for a long grueling fight with little rules to restrain the powers of the evil spirit. An exorcism consists of long sleepless periods, tormented dreams, and terrible physical pains for the exorcist. No one except a trained professional should try to conduct an exorcism.

The second form of exorcism is a tamer rite by comparison. It is performed on a house or a general area as a sort of cleansing rite. This exorcism is quite different from the first. The exorcist enters the home and begins to perform various religious prayers and blessing rites. The evil spirits are cast out of the home and other spirits cannot enter. Both exorcism rites are extremely different, but both perform basically the same function. They remove unwanted spirits.

Ghost Hunters should think long and hard about the serious consequences of getting involved in an exorcism. Hunting for ghosts is one thing, but getting involved with evil spirits and demons is something else entirely. You may endanger yourself and your family. Stop and ask yourself, "why am I doing this?" You must have an unshakable religious belief and should be a mature age. (The recommended age is over forty). You must be ready to stay awake for days at a time conducting long ritualistic prayers. You must put your own soul on the line to save the possessed person. You must also be ready to accept the danger that you may become possessed by the same demon that you are trying to cast out. If you are unable to reasonably answer those questions, or if you find that you do not fit the recommended requirements, you should not get involved in an exorcism.

(Also See: *Possession.*)

Fortean Phenomena

Fortean is the term used to describe paranormal phenomena that science can't explain. The term Fortean is named from Charles Fort (1874-1932), an American who catalogued thousands of strange phenomena that could not be explained in rational terms, which science, at the time, refused to investigate. The paranormal phenomena that Fort catalogued included unnatural rains consisting of frogs, stones, fish, dead birds, snakes, blood, or oil. Fort also investigated religious stigmata occurrences; balls of strange lights seen in the night sky, spontaneous human combustion, ghosts, poltergeists, and mysterious creatures that the world considered monsters. He catalogued literally thousands of strange events in four books that he wrote during his lifetime.

Glowing Eyes

Visitors to haunted locations with disturbingly violent or tragic histories frequently report seeing glowing eyes looking back at them in the darkness. Common locations include old prison systems, psychiatric hospitals, battlefields, and other places where daily life was a torturous existence. These locations tend to have a strong residual psychic energy lingering from past events.

There are some basic theories surrounding the origin and nature of the glowing eye phenomena. The most popular theory is that the glowing eyes are not ghosts, but are instead Nature Spirits sometimes referred to as Elementals. These spirits camp in locations where they can feed off of the residual psychic energy. Glowing eyes and residual psychic energy have a cause and effect relationship. The eyes materialize more often during peek psychic times, such as with solar flares and moon influences. Visitors with a certain amount of psychic ability observe the glowing eyes more often than someone with no psychic abilities.

Another theory is that the glowing eyes are manifested by the presence of an evil or demonic entity. The evil spirit leeches off of the negative psychic energy. In this theory, the evil spirit draws more energy from the ghosts of the location that they are holding and controlling. In most cases, the glowing eyes do not fit into the typically evil or demonic profile. The entity behind the glowing eyes seems to be more curious than malevolent. Their appearance can be frightening, but they almost always shy away from human contact. The glowing eyes have probably been mistakenly categorized as evil or demonic because they are usually associated with locations that are filled with massive amounts of negative energy.

The color of the glowing eyes can vary from location to location and even within the same spirit. The eye colors seen most frequently are yellow, blue, green, and red. (Red does not equal evil.) The eye colors do not appear to have significance to the personality or the current mood of the spirit. Instead, the color of the eyes seems to be linked directly to the natural environment and the level of residual psychic energy currently at the location.

The glowing eyes have been reported to follow and spy on visitors. Most witnesses only catch a quick glimpse of the glowing eyes before they vanish from sight. While these entities are typically nonviolent, there is always cause to take precautions. Do not go alone into areas where glowing eyes have been reported and don't attempt to contact these spirits with Ouija Boards, magic rituals, or séances.

Gray Ladies

Gray ladies are the apparitions of women who have died violently for the sake of love, been murdered by a lover, lived in an unhappy or abusive marriage, or suffered in life over the loss of a loved one. These ghosts haunt homes either waiting to be reunited with their true love or to be set free from their curse.

Gray Ladies can appear dressed in gray, white, or black. They are constantly weeping in utter sadness, longing for the love that will release them from their prisons of agony. Despite their eternal gloom, gray ladies have been credited with providing preemptive warnings of disasters that have saved the lives of many men, women, and children.

At Bolling Hall in Bradford, England, there is a mysterious bedroom called the ghost room. In 1642, a Civil War broke out. The Royalist army, under the control of Earl of Newcastle, besieged the town of Bradford. Despite not having an army and no fortification, the town held out against the Royalist Armies advances. Earl became so furious that he stood on the hillside overlooking the town and declared that the following morning he would slaughter every man, woman, and child in the town. Then, Earl went to sleep in the ghost room of the Bolling Hall. Later that night, a white lady appeared and disturbed the sleeping Earl by pulling the covers from his bed three times. The terrified Earl sat up. The ghost asked him to take pity on the town before vanishing. The next morning the Earl of Newcastle rescinded his military orders and spared the lives of hundreds of innocent townspeople.

The gray lady is one of the few ghosts that can have their pain lifted by the living. Living individuals can find the clues that will help set them free from their pain. When their stories are discovered, they will find peace. Once the real truth about their murders is uncovered and their last wishes are fulfilled, these apparitions can go onto a more peaceful existence.

Haunting

A haunting is the continuous manifestation of inexplicable phenomena associated with the presence of ghosts or spirits attached to a particular location. The most common are haunted houses, however, any place can become haunted; hotels, prisons, castles, schools, and even open fields, lakes, natural springs and man-made wells.

The term haunt comes from the same Latin root as home. Haunted locations are usually places that the deceased frequented or preferred during their lifetime. After death, the ghosts seem unable or unwilling to let go of that piece of their life. Some haunted locations involve violent or untimely deaths. Those ghosts seem to be trapped at the location unable to move on. Other haunted locations have no clear explanation. Haunts tend to be random and continuous, occurring more often on the anniversaries of deaths or special dates of importance in the past life of the ghost. Every haunt is different. They must be looked at and studied on an individual case-by-case basis to discover each of their unique characteristics.

A common misconception is that anyone visiting a haunted location will experience some kind of supernatural phenomena or see a ghost. Haunts are unpredictable. The ghosts are not there to put on a show for the living. The ghosts make their presence known on their time, not ours. A ghost hunter may have to visit an alleged haunt dozens of times before finding any evidence of paranormal activity.

Haunts revolve completely around human sensory perceptions, (sight, sound, touch, taste, and smell). A typical haunting will involve strange noises, such as slamming doors, loud thumps, tapping sounds, and unexplained footsteps. Smells may include perfumes or colognes worn by the deceased or the smell of their favorite flowers. They may also be repulsive odors like the smell of rotting flesh. Sensations of prickling on the skin or hot and cold spots are commonly reported. There are the feelings of being touched or pushed by unseen hands. Some rare haunts experience the destructive nature of a poltergeist. Broken household objects, vanishing personal items, and rearranged furniture are a few of the poltergeist characteristics haunts sometimes tend to share.

The sighting of a ghost in a haunting is extremely rare, but not completely uncommon. The manifestation and demeanor of each apparition will vary. Some ghosts will appear exactly as they did in life, even wearing the same period clothing. For example, ghosts of the American Civil War are often seen in locations relating to the war still wearing their uniforms. A few ghostly soldiers even have blood-soaked bandages wrapped around their fatal wounds.

The patterns that apparitions follow will also differ from case to case. Some ghosts will not, or cannot acknowledge the presence of the living. They seem to be eternally reenacting events from their own daily life. These types of haunts are called atmospheric or residual. Seeing these ghosts is much like watching a window in history.

Some haunting ghosts can make eye contact or give a simple head nod to the living to acknowledge their presence, but will not let it interfere with their task.

Other ghosts seem to be in desperate need to communicate with the living, going out of their way to make their presence known and felt.

Haunting ghosts may appear as real people, undistinguishable from another living person. Witnesses have told stories of meeting, shaking hands, and having conversations with other individuals only to discover later that they had actually met a ghost. A majority of ghosts, however, appear fuzzy and transparent with shades of a white or gray color. Some visions of ghosts appear horrific and terrifying, such as rotten corpses, disfigured forms, or headless bodies.

In almost every haunting, the ghosts are not violent and do not have any malicious tendencies. If there is a violent nature to the haunt, the case must be made that it is not really a haunting. It is probably a poltergeist or the workings of some other supernatural force. Ghosts of deceased individuals are not the only spirits known to haunt. Phantom cats, dogs, horses, even bears and pigs have been reported in haunted areas. Objects can also be haunted.

Ley Lines and Power Points

Ley Lines are the invisible alignments between sacred or mystical locations, which are usually built on sites with energy vortexes. Because the energy from vortexes is electromagnetic, the energies push and pull against each other just like the attraction of magnets. The pathways in-between sacred locations often have much more paranormal activity then other surrounding areas. These sacred sites can be very short distances from each other or hundreds of miles apart.

When sacred sites or energy vortexes are plotted on an area map, the straight lines connecting these locations are the Ley Lines. Sacred sites can include churches, temples, megaliths, burial sites, springs, shrines, bridges, stone circles, legendary trees, battlefields, forts, holy wells, graves, earth mounds, and basically any location with a spiritual or magical significance.

The unseen energy flowing through these invisible lines influences the environment and boosts paranormal activity. When multiple sacred sites are clustered together, the intersection points of crossing Ley Lines becomes a focal point of powerful energy and paranormal activity. Power Points can be described as spiraling rhythms of earth energy being drawn together from different sources to form a concentrated energy mass. Power Points have abnormal amounts of ghost and UFO sightings and poltergeist activity making them a focus for many paranormal investigations.

Marian Apparitions

Marian apparitions are the appearances of the Blessed Virgin Mary. Despite the numerous reports around the world of the appearance of the Virgin Mary, the Catholic Church, who solely investigates these sightings, has only confirmed a handful as genuine.

The Marian apparition consists of the manifestation of a beautiful luminous woman who identifies herself as Mary. She delivers a spiritual message to the witnesses and asks for more churches and virgin shrines to be erected in her name. Her message is always that of peace, love, and a better understanding of God and the teachings of Jesus.

One or more of the following usually accompany the apparition of the Virgin Mary: incredible unexplained lights that glow and spin in the sky, brilliant crosses that hover over the witnesses in the heavens, sounds of beautiful music, and the sweet smell of incense.

Some witnesses to the Marian phenomena fall into a trance state where they receive spiritual guidance, healing of maladies, and messages. One of the most famous Marian apparitions ever recorded began in 1981 in the village of Medjugorje, Bosnia, where six young children began seeing visions of the Virgin Mary. By 1985, the children had received over two thousand sightings and hundreds of spontaneous healings had occurred. Thousands of believers and non-believers flocked to the village. Almost all of them saw, felt, or experienced something that they could not explain in rational terms.

Marian apparitions can also occur in other forms, such as Virgin statues that cry tears of blood or the silhouette or face of Mary appearing on natural or manmade objects. Despite these visions, the Catholic Church retains the view that these apparitions are not ghosts, but in fact are amazing spiritual events that are allowed to happen by God.

Nature Spirits (Sometimes referred to as *Elementals*.)

Nature spirits can be various types of beings. They can either be the four elements of earth, air, water, and fire. Or, they can be magical creatures that inhabit secluded natural environments. Elves, fairies, trolls, pixies, sprites, goblins, kobolds, gnomes, and brownies are some of the countless nature spirits that children grow up knowing as characters in fairy tales.

Nature spirits usually have animalistic appearances and special magical abilities. They have the power to remain invisible to human eyes. They are only seen when they want to be seen or when a magic spell has been cast over them. They are believed to keep a certain balance in nature.

Phantom Animals

The ghosts of common household pets have been known to return home from time-to-time. Their collars can be heard jingling. Barks and meows echo loudly through empty rooms and they can manifest in solid or transparent forms, just like any other ghost. The most common of the phantom animals are dogs, cats, birds and horses, but it does seem that any type of animal can become a ghost. There are reports of ghostly wild bears and farm animals that include sheep, cows, mules, chickens, and pigs.

Phantom animals generally haunt the places that they knew in life the same as traditional ghosts. People have even told stories of the ghostly pet climbing into bed and cuddling up next to them at night.

There are some phantom occurrences that are not friendly. There are many stories of phantom dogs and felines terrorizing people by chasing them from pet cemeteries, making horrible noises, and attacking anyone that does not run from them. There is a theory that suggests the owners give their pets souls through all of the love and affection that they give to them. This is an interesting theory, but it does not seem to hold up in every case. There are cases when the phantom animals did not have an owner, such as the ghosts of wild animals. There are also instances where the phantom animals did not receive love from a caring home, but just the opposite. They were tortured and badly mistreated throughout their lives.

Phantom Hounds

Throughout the ages there have been reports of large supernatural black dogs that are sinister and vicious. They are normally much larger than the average canine and have fierce red glowing eyes. These phantom dogs appear in folklore tales and legends as death omens and are associated with the devil. They are sometimes accompanied by a dark hooded figure, which is said to be Satan himself.

Phantom hounds tend to manifest primarily in old churchyards, cemeteries, and on lonely hillsides and roadways. Appearing more often on stormy nights and full moons, they chase away anyone that happens to cross paths with them. British legends tell of packs of these demon dogs that run with no heads. Their red glowing eyes appear in the spots where they would be. They are ominous and intimidating. The people that report seeing them suffer from traumatizing shock.

The beasts leave no footprints and run silently with no sound of their passing. The only sound that can be heard is from their icy breath and taunting howls that echo across the hillsides. Terrified travelers have raced for their lives from these beasts. When the phantom hounds reach the edge of their domain, they vanish into thin air leaving behind only a fading angry growl.

The appearances of phantom hounds seem to be at random. Sometimes manifesting to guard something of importance, such as a sacred artifact, sacred location, or to protect their sleeping master. They are considered to be an evil or demonic force, prowling their haunts searching for lost travelers or unsuspecting intruders to terrorize. Phantom hounds have also been reported to run out in front of vehicles at night and disappear just before the vehicle hits them.

While run-ins with phantom dogs are extremely frightening, they are seldom deadly. In almost all cases recorded throughout history, everyone that saw these monsters was able to out run them and make it to safety. This leads many investigators to conclude that phantom hounds cannot hurt people, because there is simply no way that these strong, giant beasts would not be able to catch the average person in a foot race. However, there is a British legend that says if you see a phantom dog for the third time, it will kill. Deaths and injuries tend to occur from the actions that people take while being chased. In states of utter panic, people jump or fall from cliff edges or drive off the road crashing their cars.

Phantom hounds are also referred to as the hateful things, churchyard beasts, church raiders, cemetery guardians, black shuck, black dogs, hell beasts, Cerberus, and hellhounds.

Phantom Hitchhikers

One of the most common phantom encounters is that of the phantom hitchhiker. These stories are so widespread that there is virtually no culture in the world that does not have some kind of variation on this paranormal encounter.

As the stories go…

A woman hitchhiker, alone and sometimes-in distress, is seen standing at the side of the road late at night by a male driver. The woman is young, 16-25 years of age, and usually wearing all white. The driver stops to ask if she needs a ride. After a brief conversation where they exchange names, she tells the driver her home address. The driver agrees to take her home because it's usually on his way. The female hitchhiker gets in the car and the real ghost story begins. Sometimes, the driver gives the woman his coat or a blanket to keep warm. She rarely says another word for the entire trip, but the driver can't help notice her incredible beauty.

The story can end differently depending on who is telling the story. Sometimes the hitchhiker remains in the car until the driver reaches her house. The man then suddenly discovers that she is gone, vanished from the car. In his confusion, the driver knocks on the front door of the house. He explains the events of his strange night to the family, only to be told that the woman he picked up sounds a lot like their deceased daughter. The daughter has usually been killed, murdered, or died in a tragic car accident at the exact spot where the driver found her only hours ago. After the parents show the driver a picture of their daughter, he identifies the girl as the hitchhiker. The story ends with the driver eventually going to visit the gravesite of the girl where he finds his coat or blanket draped over her tombstone.

There are other stories where the hitchhiker needs to get to a dance or special party. The driver agrees to escort the girl. They arrive at the dance and have a wonderful time together. On the way back home, the girl tells the driver to go past the local graveyard. She thanks the driver for a fantastic evening that she'll never forget. As the driver passes the graveyard, the girl mysteriously vanishes. After asking some questions the next day, the driver discovers that a girl with the same name had died on the way to that dance many years ago. She was now buried in the graveyard that they passed right before she disappeared from the moving car.

Most of these phantom hitchhiker stories occur on the anniversary of the ghost's mortal death. Whether or not these legends are true or some form of hallucination, urban legend, or prank remains an unsolved mystery.

Phantom Ships

Phantom ships have terrified sailors for hundreds of years. The most common sightings occur as phantom ships recreate the event that doomed them, usually crashing violently during a storm. Countless humans have lost their lives because of shipwrecks and the phantom ships seem to echo that horror.

The appearance of phantom ships is thought to be a death omen by sailors. Strange circumstances; fires, sinking, and sudden fierce storms tend to coincide with their sightings. Despite the superstition, many crews that have seen phantom ships have returned to tell about them. When a British ship saw the famous phantom ship, The Flying Dutchman, they feared that it was going to collide with them, but the ship passed by and a massive storm began. When the H.M.S. Bacchante encountered the Flying Dutchman in 1881, tragedy befell the crew when one of the crewmembers fell from the rigging to his death.

Ghost ships include all kinds of seaworthy vessels. Pirate ships, shipping vessels, pleasure boats, and military warships have all been seen sailing on without crews. Some reports even include the physical boarding of ghost ships. Everything onboard was found to be intact and good working order despite the fact that no crewmembers could be located. The ships were always lost sight of later, when massive thunderstorms left the living crewmembers fighting for their own ship's life.

Phantom ships have also been seen hovering in the fog and flying over the water. Some of the most famous phantom ships include The Flying Dutchman, which sunk in The Cape of Good Hope, and the Griffon, which can still be seen drifting in the waters of the Great Lakes. More detail on Phantom ships can be read in the **Famous Ghost Stories** chapter.

Phantom Travelers

Phantom travelers are ghosts that haunt traveled routes. These doomed souls are usually of victims of a tragic death that happened along the same path. These phantoms haunt with powerful emotion, sometimes leading the unsuspecting lost traveler to his or her own terrible death. Popular ghost stories place phantom travelers everywhere from less traveled country roads to major airports and railway stations.

This type of phantom can be male or female, moving in both solid and transparent forms. They float along with the dense midnight fog, walk alone down dark roads, ride ghostly horses across the countryside, or drive in phantom cars. Witnesses have reported hitting phantom travelers head-on with their vehicles only to discover that the car passed straight though the phantom before it vanished. Their mission on this earthly realm remains an elusive mystery. They seem violently angry about their own deaths and are willing to take their anger out on any unlucky individual.

The majority of phantom travelers only make one appearance per year, on the anniversary of their death. Many airports have reported the unexplained appearances of passengers who have been killed in plane accidents, asking about their flight and luggage. It can be quite a chilling experience for the workers. One railroad station reported that riders waiting for their train occasionally get the gory and traumatizing treat of seeing a phantom  reenactment of a man who committed suicide by jumping in front of a speeding train. In some of these cases, unexplained bursts of light have been recorded on video surveillance cameras during visits by phantom travelers in public areas.

The places where the ghosts of phantom travelers linger are extremely haunted. The routes exhibit strange occurrences including bright lights, loud accident sounds like crashing and twisting metal, and intense screams of agony.

Poltergeist Activity

A poltergeist is a malevolent form of psychokinetic energy, which manifests with paranormal characteristics. The word poltergeist is a German word, which literally translated means, *noisy spirit*.

The earliest known reports of poltergeists date back to the ancient Romans, in which poltergeists threw stones at travelers. Other poltergeist records can be found in the medieval times of China and Germany. The reports indicate unexplainable events such as flying dirt or other objects, awful smells, loud noises, unexplained lights, and ghostly apparitions. All of which are very similar to the still ongoing reports of modern poltergeists. The exact reason poltergeist activity occurs has been under debate by experts for decades. Poltergeists usually begin and end abruptly. The typical incident can last for several hours or several years.

There have been hundreds of independent studies done on poltergeists. A majority of the cases revolve around an individual or agent, as they are called. The phenomenon seems to be linked to a type of subconscious psychokinesis (PK) on the part of the agent. University studies in Parapsychology have discovered that most of the poltergeist agents are females under the age of twenty who are totally unaware that they are involuntarily directing the poltergeist energy.

Parapsychology investigations have uncovered a link between the agents and states of poor mental or physical health. Emotional problems associated with agent personalities are anxiety, hysteria, anger, obsessions, phobias, and schizophrenia. In some cases, with psychological help to relieve the emotional tensions, the poltergeist energies diminish and disappear.

It should be pointed out that while a majority of poltergeists revolve around mentally unstable human agents, there are cases where all of the people involved are psychologically stable and seem to have no control over the poltergeist energy. These cases remain a mystery. Some paranormal researchers blame them on other supernatural forces including ghosts, spirits, and even evil or demonic influences.

The differences between poltergeist activity and a haunting can be very hard to distinguish. In the early stages of a poltergeist, it may be impossible to differentiate it from a haunting. Haunts and poltergeists do share basic aspects, (apparitions, strange noises, odors, moving or disappearing objects, etc.), however, there are some characteristics that drastically separate the two.

Ways that Haunts and Poltergeists Differ:

Haunting: Involves the ghosts of deceased human beings appearing frequently in certain places and times.
Poltergeist: May not be ghosts at all. There are theories that poltergeists are mass forms of PK energy that a living person is unknowingly controlling. In some cases, extreme poltergeist activity has been linked to evil spirits and demons.

Haunting: The appearance of ghosts is in areas known to the deceased before death.
Poltergeist: Can be triggered by a living person's trauma in any location, at any time.

Haunting: Activities are continuous over time, concentrated in the same general location.
Poltergeist: Activities build up over time to a climax and then start over. Poltergeist energies can travel anywhere with anyone.

Haunting: Are not violent by nature.
Poltergeist: Nearing the climax of the energy cycle, poltergeists can become dangerous, inflicting both mental and physical terror in extreme cases.

Five Levels of a Poltergeist:

This chart goes by levels that are accumulative as they progress. That means for example, that level 3 poltergeists will have all the characteristics of a level 3, but also exhibit the characteristics of levels 1 and 2. This chart is an ongoing experiment developed by the book's author. It may need to be updated or altered when new research information becomes available.

LEVEL 1: The Sense Attack

Level 1 is referred to as The Sense Attack because, in the early stages, the poltergeist revolves mainly around the basic human senses. Individuals experiencing this stage of a poltergeist might hear strange noises in the middle of the night or walk into a room and feel an unexplained cold spot move over their body. They might smell strange odors that seem to have no source or see shadows move and lights flicker. Pet activity should be monitored. Animals tend to have a "sixth sense" when it comes to the supernatural.

Characteristics: Cold or Hot Spots- Strange Noises (knocking sounds, etc.) - Odd Smells or Offensive Odors - Unusual Animal Activity (dogs/cats running from rooms, etc.) - Feelings of Being Watched.

LEVEL 2: Communication

At this level of a poltergeist, noises, smells, and odors become more direct. The poltergeist is still in the basic energy stages, but the intensity is turned up a few notches. The encounters that were experienced in the first stage will change. Instead of hearing indefinable noises, the noises will change into whispers or giggles. Instead of feeling cold spots, cold air will rush through rooms like the wind. Small marks or symbols can be discovered on walls, floors, or ceilings. Objects and furniture will begin to mysteriously move, seemingly, under their own power. Unseen hands throw small objects. This is the poltergeist's way of communicating its presence to the living.

Characteristics: Whispers, Laughs, Giggles, Moans or Shrieking - Moving Shadows - Breezes in Closed Areas - Visible Clouds (base apparition) - Stronger than Normal Static Electricity - Marks on the Floors or Walls- Objects that have Moved or are Thrown.

LEVEL 3: Electrical Control

At this stage the poltergeist begins to make its presence felt. The difference in the first two levels is that the events can be explained away as the mind playing tricks or natural causes. At this stage, it is hard not to notice that something very real is happening. This is also the level of the classic haunting. People living in a house where poltergeist energies reach this level begin to become afraid. They come to the conclusion that something paranormal is happening. Fear takes over as the main emotion. This fear seems to fuel the poltergeist. It feeds on the fear to move onto the next level.

Characteristics: Lights and other Electrical Appliances Turning On/Off - Unseen Hands Grabbing and/or Touching People - Writings on Walls or Pattern Markings - Doors and Windows that Open/Close or Lock/Unlock - Hearing Voices - Full Apparitions/Dark Figures - Direct Communication with Apparitions - Strange Phone Calls - Falling Objects - Moving Furniture.

LEVEL 4: The Trickster Stage

This is the stage where an advanced poltergeist begins to gain momentum, much like a snowball rolling downhill. The poltergeist develops at a more rapid rate, always moving closer to the danger level and continuing to pick up a clearer sense of consciousness. At this stage, objects disappear or are hurled across the room. Furniture violently shakes. Trash cans and household objects spontaneously burst into flames. Unseen forces violently push people. Scary voices shout out obscenities and order the living to leave. Sometimes, it may seem as if a playful ghost is doing the actions at this stage. However, if it is a poltergeist, it may be gathering knowledge of what the people around it consider frightening. At the next level, it will use the information gained in a malicious and violent manner to create an atmosphere of absolute terror, which it then will use to feed from and build its own energy.

Characteristics: Flying/Moving Objects - Objects Disappearing/Reappearing - Violently Shaking Furniture - Spontaneous Fires - Apparitions Appearing as Frightening Entities - Unseen Forces Pushing or Shaking People - Visions or Illusions - Voices Speaking in Ordering Tones/Foul Language - People Feeling Dizzy or Nauseated - Windows, Mirrors, or Other Household Objects Shatter for No Reason - Levitation - Physical Attacks.

LEVEL 5: The Danger Level

At this level the poltergeist is at its highest energy point and should be considered dangerous. Serious violent and life-threatening actions usually occur at this stage. This level can be horrifying to all of the living members involved. The time frame here, and with all the stages listed, will vary depending on the poltergeist. It could end in days, months, or even years. At the end of this stage, the poltergeist will go dormant for an unknown period of time and then begin this cycle over again starting back at the first level. This stage will involve violent physical attacks involving brutal injuries. Biting, scratching, punching, and sexual assaults may occur. Dangerous household objects such as sharp kitchen knives fly across rooms aimed to spear individuals. Blazing fires start up in rooms when everyone is asleep. The poltergeist energy does everything it can to lash out against the individual in its environment.

Characteristics: Dangerous Activity - Biting, Slapping, Punching, or Hair Pulling - Animated Objects (Jewelry, dolls, furniture)- Human Possession - Use of Household Electrical Systems to Cause Harm - Fires - Blood on Walls, Floors, Ceiling - Vicious Attacks by Unseen Forces - Being Held Down - Sexual Assaults - Flying Knives or Other Sharp Objects - Heavy Objects Falling Over with the Intent to Kill - Threatening Writings and Marks - Threatening Voices.

If you feel that you are encountering poltergeist activity, do not wait to look for help. If you think that the poltergeist is linked to an object in your possession, get rid of that object right away. Do not try to move or run away from a poltergeist. Running is a waste of time. If the poltergeist is linked to a person or object, it will follow right along with you. The best thing to do is seek out professional help as soon as you can. It should not cost you a penny to do so. If you find someone that wants to charge you a fee, look for someone else.

Possession

Possession is when a person's mind and body is taken over by ghosts, spirits, or demons.

There are three forms of possession. The first form is when an evil spirit or demon directly enters a person and takes complete control over their mind and body. The second is when a magic user, such as a wizard or witch, commands a spirit to enter the body of another person. The last is when a person voluntarily allows a spirit to enter their body for a given period of time.

Possession, for the most part, is considered to be an act of the devil. For the possessed person, or host, the experience is painful and traumatic. Both psychological and religious help is needed to free a person from the grips of a possession. A holy man can perform the religious rite of exorcism to cast out the evil spirits from the host. Psychotherapists should also be contacted to conduct a patient mental health evaluation. Many possession cases are actually misdiagnosed mental illnesses. If the patient is considered to be in good mental and physical health prior to and after the possession, it will still be necessary to consult with a psychologist for post trauma therapy. Possession experiences can leave deep emotional scars that may resurface later in life.

Some initial warning signs of possession include migraine headaches, violent sickness, sleep disorders, strange noises or lights, unexplained whispers and voices, poltergeist activity, and bouts of temporary insanity. In the advanced stages of the possession, expect to observe severe physical appearance changes in the host. Psychic abilities, abnormal physical strength, blasphemy, self-mutilation, levitation, speaking in foreign tongues, and the appearance of strange marks either on walls, household objects, or on the skin of the host are also early warning signs.

Possession experiences can last for days, months, or years. In some cases, the invading spirits are unwilling to set their host free and seem very happy to torture and torment the living until the host body finally dies. Only an experienced holy man, not a ghost hunter, should handle possession cases. Seek out professional assistance. The Catholic Church is among the few religious bodies still conducting exorcisms.

Schizophrenia, paranoia, hysteria, and multiple personality disorders are some of the psychological disorders that are commonly mistaken for possession.

(Also See: *Exorcism*.)

Psychic Attacks

Psychic attacks are paranormal assaults on humans or animals that can cause physical or mental distress, illness, bodily injury, and death. They are a kind of sorcery with the equivalent power of a curse. They can be performed in many ways, from magic rituals and voodoo dolls, to human willpower and out-of-body projections. There can be psychic attacks from otherworldly entities such as ghosts, spirits, and demons.

The victims of psychic attacks can experience simple periods of bad luck and skin rashes to full-blown diseases and life threatening accidents. Some victims seem to have their soul, or life force, slowly drained away as in cases of psychic vampirism. The victims lose all will to live and gradually deteriorate until death. After death, doctors tend to be at a loss for an exact cause of death.

Psychic vampires claim to be able to use their psychic powers to inflict harm on other people. They use their paranormal powers to suck the life force away from someone else, much like a regular vampire does, but without the biting. A psychic vampire can drain small amounts of energy or they can completely drain their victims until death. The real power of this paranormal entity is that it is almost impossible to distinguish the effects of a common illness from a case of psychic vampirism. In most cases of psychic attacks, the mere suggestion of an attack is enough to cause personal problems like paranoia, hysteria, and nervous breakdowns.

Retrocognition (Sometimes referred to as *Postcognition*.)

Retrocognition is a spontaneous vision of the past usually manifesting as a hallucination or dream-like vision. It is a radical theory that involves the displacement of time letting an individual witness past events as they actually happened. Retrocognition is difficult to test in laboratory settings because it is scientifically impossible to prove or disprove these events when dealing with existing historical events.

Retrocognition is thought to be a significant factor in ghost sightings and haunts. Some paranormal researchers go as far as to say that a majority of apparitions observed are actually cases of spontaneous Retrocognition. The witnesses are not actually seeing ghosts, but actual, real life events from the past.

Séance

Séances are private meetings conducted by a medium for the purpose of communicating with the spirits of the dead. Séances are typically held inside the home of the medium. Individuals sit around a table and hold hands with the person next to them. The medium then induces a trance-like state, making their body more open to the spiritual world. The medium's trance lets the supernatural entities enter their body and communicate to the audience through them. The entities can speak, write, or manifest for the audience through the medium.

The materialization of ectoplasm is a common part of a séance. The spirits, allegedly, produce ectoplasm and it flows from the body of the medium. It may exit from their nose, eyes, mouth, ears, underarms, or private parts.

For the most part, séances and the mediums that conduct them are frauds. Spiritualists have used séances for several decades to turn a quick buck by taking advantage of emotionally vulnerable individuals. The fraudulent mediums prey on grieving individuals who have lost loved ones. They fool these vulnerable people into believing that they alone can communicate with the deceased loved one.

The false medium gathers some of the mourners together and pretends to conjure the ghost of the loved one that has passed. The entire process can be rather elaborate, sometimes consisting of moving furniture, flashing lights, and strange sounds. All these illusions are rigged-up by mechanical devices, wires, and other common magic tricks. While being rather dramatic, the frauds use relatively simple illusions such as slight-of-hand tricks and eye diversions to take the attention away from what they are really doing. The mediums then pretend to be possessed by the spirits and either speak for them or write down messages from the spirit.

Impartial witnesses to séances usually have no problems discovering the methods of fraud used by the mediums in only a few minutes. This is why it is very hard to find a medium that will conduct a séance with scientists or ghost hunters present. Their reasoning is that a skeptical mind will contaminate the séance or that they are not conducting the séance to prove the existence of ghosts. The truth is that 99 percent of séances are conducted by fraudulent mediums that do not want their secrets exposed.

Soul

The term *soul* is defined differently by each of the major religions. The soul seems to be the spiritual life force or essence of being, carrying an individual's personality. The soul is a person's conscious identity.

Most religions seem to share the belief that the soul and the body are two separate entities. The mortal physical body is no more than a fleshy vessel for the soul. After death, the soul has the ability to detach from the body and move onto other planes of existence.

The appearances of a ghost are said to be the soul of the deceased appearing from the invisible spiritual realm. The form of the appearance can look exactly as it did before death or take other forms from the different stages of life. It is the belief in many religions, such as Buddhism and Hinduism that the soul can be reincarnated into a new human body or animal. (See: *Reincarnation*.)

Spirit

The term *spirit* is often used to describe the soul, however, spirits can take on forms and meanings beyond the definition of the soul. Spirits can include the forces of nature. They can represent places, objects, and other non-living things, such as the spirit of a lake, a forest, or the spirit of a sacred shrine. Spirits can also come in the forms of fairies, elves, and other forest elemental beings.

Ghosts tend to appear in human form, while spirits appear as patterns of formless bright light or energy. If the soul is the identity, the spirit is the willpower and driving force behind the soul.

Telephone Calls From The Dead

Try to imagine the following:

The telephone rings. You pick up the receiver and say hello. A familiar voice answers and continues to talk. This would be a typical experience except the caller is a close friend that passed away the week before. They tell you that they are fine and that you shouldn't worry about them. Before you can get the nerve to say anything, the call slowly fades out leaving the line silent. You listen for a few more seconds before hanging up the phone in total shock.

While being a rare form of spirit communication, there have been hundreds of reports of this mysterious phenomenon, named simply, telephone calls from the dead.

In almost all of these cases, the phantom caller has a close emotional tie with the contact. They are usually a spouse, parent, child, or good friend. The intentions of the telephone call will vary. Sometimes the calls will be on the date of a special anniversary or to warn of some kind of impending danger. Other times, the telephone calls are messages for the living to carry out a task on behalf of the deceased. The majority of these phantom calls seem to be to express love and to say a final goodbye.

The phantom caller's voice sounds exactly the same as when they were alive. There may be static or other strange noises on the line. The telephone calls can last from a few seconds to a couple of minutes. The conversation usually ends with the phantom voice fading away until there is nothing to be heard on the line but an eerie silence.

Critics point out that these cases are probably dreams or hallucinations. Others have concluded that this is one way that the human psyche deals with the loss of a close loved one; a way of working out the intense feelings felt from a tragic loss. To an extent, the critics have valid points, however, it should be noted that a percentage of these contacts had no idea that the person calling them was even dead until after the fact.

This type of spirit communication has also been reported in other electrical appliances such as radios, CB's, television sets, and computer systems.

Vampires

Vampires are demons that inhabit the undead body of a resurrected corpse. The vampire stalks the night feeding off of the living by drinking their lifeblood before returning to the grave at sunrise. Vampirism is like an infectious disease, spreading from vampire to victim. Almost all cultures of the world have held a belief in vampires in one form or another. Vampires have been called, Vampir in Hungary, Upior in Poland, Wampira by Russians, and Nosferatu in Romania, which actually means *undead* or *disease carrier*.

Vampire victims in the early stages of vampirism can be easily detected by their uncharacteristic and sometimes violent mood swings, their blasphemous tongue, an aversion to sunlight, sudden illnesses, decaying flesh, abnormal strength, physical changes (such as the growth of sharp teeth), and finally, a new lust for blood. Animals can also be infected with the vampirism disease. There have been reports of vampire cats, dogs, wolves, and even simple farm animals.

The earliest known legends, dating back centuries, suggest that vampires were nomadic, moving from place to place to conceal their identities. This nomadic lifestyle led to the misinterpretation that vampires must be gypsies. The vampire tales would all begin in the same manner. Village farm animals would start to disappear and turn up dead with all of their blood drained. Then, villagers would begin to unexpectedly fall ill and die mysteriously. Madness and paranoia would engulf the small communities until the tide of unexplained deaths passed. Then, stories of the dead villagers rising from their graves would flood the peaceful communities. Many cultures took the threat of vampirism very seriously and took any step deemed necessary to combat and prevent these unholy abominations from invading their towns.

Vampires can take on human form, almost passing as normal, except for their skin color, which is always a pale white due to the fact that no blood flows through their undead bodies. Vampires have no pulse, and no soul. They can shape-shift into wolves, bats, and other monstrous creatures of the night. The have psychic powers over their victims and powerful influences.

Even with all of their supernatural powers, vampires have weaknesses that can be used to destroy them. Sunlight will cause vampires to burn up and explode into balls of fire. A wooden, iron, or silver stake through the heart will destroy them. Chopping off a vampire's head will also destroy it. Crucifixes, religious symbols, and holy water are said to inflict great pain and suffering on these unholy beasts.

Despite the glamorous depictions of vampires that have been portrayed in recent novels and movies, the early historical vampire accounts describe them as inhuman, foul smelling, gruesome monsters. Savage brutes, that murdered, drank blood, and feasted on human flesh in the shadowy darkness. The vicious attacks by vampires left their victims almost unrecognizable. Vampires were considered to be one the lowest form of demons and were constantly being blamed for sickness, diseases, plagues, and many other human ills.

Wild Hunt

The Wild Hunt is composed of armies of spectral horsemen who ride black warhorses across midnight skies followed by vicious packs of phantom hounds. The sound of horse's hooves can be heard trampling through the air like thunder as they ride toward the unknown.

Any unlucky person who sees the Wild Hunt is transported to far away foreign lands. Anyone who speaks with one of the horseman is doomed to die. British folklore warns that anyone caught by the hounds will have their flesh devoured and soul stolen.

Christian folklore tells that the horsemen are packs of demons led by Satan himself and that the hounds are a procession of fierce hellhounds. The appearance of the Wild Hunt is more common on the night of All Hallows Eve (Halloween), the night when both the psychical realm and spirit worlds can become cross together.

It was believed, for a period in the middle ages, that it was the fate of the non-baptized souls to ride in the Wild Hunt. Souls that where not buried in holy grounds were also doomed to become part of The Hunt. The Wild Hunt is mainly ancient British Folklore, but there have been alleged sightings up to present times.

Famous Ghost Stories

Haunted Locations

Borley Rectory - Essex, England

The Borley Rectory has the ominous reputation of being, "the most haunted house in England." The Reverend Henry Dawson Ellis Bull built the Rectory in 1863, but previously, it was the site of a much older monastery built by Benedictine Monks in 1362. Located across the road from the Rectory is an even older church dating back to 1066, which, at the time, consisted of only a small wooden frame. Paranormal investigators who study the Borley Rectory have come to the conclusion that its violent and tragic history doomed the Rectory to become haunted.

The tragic history begins with an early legend. A monk from the old monastery and a nun from the nearby Bures nunnery had secretly fallen in love and were planning to elope. They well knew the harsh penalties of the church if anyone were to prove true the rumors of their relationship. The lovers planned their escape and got a friend to drive a getaway carriage for them. However, their plans went awry and the carriage was stopped. The monk was hanged as a penalty for their sin and the nun was bricked up alive inside the walls of the nunnery. Their accomplice getaway driver was beheaded. Reports of stones thrown by unseen hands began soon after these horrible events. A phantom nun began appearing on the grounds, often in broad daylight. As witnesses made an attempt to approach the nun, she always vanished right before their eyes. The phantom nun has appeared more than any other ghost at the Borley Rectory and even got a stretch of ground named after her called The Nun's Walk.

Some three hundred years later, Reverend Henry Dawson Ellis Bull built the Rectory and lived there with his wife, Caroline Sarah Foyster, where they had four children. Henry continued to add onto the Rectory over the years. He even built a summerhouse overlooking the Nun's Walk to watch the ghostly manifestations. However, the phantom nun soon became more of a problem for the Reverend and his family as it became increasingly difficult to keep working servants to stay. The haunting began to intensify and Harry Bull, the younger son of Henry, began seeing a phantom horse carriage racing up the Rectory drive. Bull's young daughters saw the ghost nun several times. Phantom rapping noises, unexplained footsteps, and the appearance of other shadowy ghosts became a regular occurrence. For many years, the children, Harry in particular, claimed that they could communicate with the spirits living in the house.

Henry Bull died in the Rectory's Blue Room on May 7, 1892. Many of the paranormal events in the home focused on the Blue Room, which already had strange phenomena. A young girl could be heard screaming from inside the room, but servants and family members would find the room completely empty. It is legend that a young girl fell or was dropped from the Blue Room window and died. A few decades later, the Blue Room would claim another soul when on June 9, 1927, Harry Bull died after being poisoned by Ivy, his wife. After Harry's death, the Rectory sat empty for several months. During this time Fred Cartwright, a local carpenter, said that he saw the phantom nun four separate times standing at the Rectory gate.

On October 2, 1928, Reverend Guy Eric Smith and his wife moved into the Borley Rectory, and they quickly realized as well that something bizarre was happening. They began hearing strange whispers and unexplained footsteps in the middle of the night. Objects were hurled at unsuspecting guests. Bright illuminations would shine from unlit rooms and two housemaids reported that they saw the phantom nun on several different occasions. The poltergeist activity continued to intensify. House keys began to disappear and small pebbles were being thrown outside at visitors. The appearance of the phantom carriage seemed to be the last straw. Fear drove the Smith family out of the Rectory.

Later that same year, the Reverend Lionel Algernon Foyster, his wife Marianne, and their daughter, Adelaide, moved into the Rectory. The poltergeist activity in the Rectory increased to a violent level when Marianne became the target of several attacks. She was maliciously punched, slapped, and scratched. This marked the most publicized period in the Borley Rectory case because Harry Price, famed psychic researcher, had been investigating the paranormal incidences and reporting his findings to the world. This time period was filled with the most activity and was also the most dangerous time at the Rectory. Objects were violently smashed and unseen forces were hurling stones at visitors. Strange writings began to appear on the walls. The writings drew suspicion and were thought to be a hoax until they began appearing while many different witnesses were in the room watching. Despite the best attempts at communication, most of the writings remain unintelligible. Two that were somewhat readable said, "Marianne, please help get" and another, "Pleas for help and prayers."

The Foyster's continued to live at the Rectory until Lionel's ill health made it impossible for him to work. The family made the decision to move from the Rectory. Shortly after the family vacated, Lionel died and Marianne married an American G.I. leaving England for America. It is a rumor that Marianne had poisoned Lionel.

After the Foyster's moved out, Harry Price picked up a one-year lease on the property and continued to study the paranormal activity. The strange events were so amazing that Price advertised jobs in The Times, the local newspaper, for trustworthy assistants to spend nights inside the Rectory to continue his investigation. The response to the ad was tremendous. Now, with a small army of forty-eight outside observers, Harry Price logged an extraordinary number of poltergeist phenomena. One peculiar event took place at a séance held on March 27th, 1938. An alleged ghost communicating from beyond the grave made two claims. The ghost claimed that a fire would start in the hallway that night and burn the Rectory to the ground and that a nun's body would be discovered in the burned ruins. Despite these extraordinary claims, nothing happened to the Rectory that night.

Harry Price proceeded with his studies estimating, "that at least two thousand poltergeist phenomena were experienced at the Rectory between October 1930 and October 1935." This time period capped off 130 years of documented unexplained paranormal activity. Price said, "Every person who has resided in the rectory since it was built in 1863, and practically every person who has taken the trouble to investigate the alleged miracles' for himself, has sworn to incidents that can only be described as paranormal."

When the one-year lease was up, the Borley Rectory was taken over by Captain WH Gregson. The Captain was also subjected to continuing poltergeist activity, including the strange disappearance of his two dogs. Eleven months to the day of the ghostly séance premonitions, a book fell from a bookshelf in the hallway knocking over an oil lamp, which started a fire. The blaze spread too quickly to stop. Moments later, the Rectory was completely engulfed in flames. Local witnesses who gathered to watch the Rectory burn claimed to see ghostly figures roaming through the fire-lit rooms. Many witnesses said that they saw a phantom nun peering down from an upstairs window.

Harry Price returned to the Rectory once again in 1943 determined to uncover the truth. He dug deep into the cellar floor and discovered the jawbone of a young woman. Price was convinced that this jawbone was part of the nun's skeleton. Thus, validating both séance predictions of a fire destroying the Rectory and of a nun being found in the building's remains. Price speculated that the nun needed to have a Christian burial to put her spirit at rest, but his attempts must have failed because the phantom nun is still an active apparition.

The Rectory building was demolished in 1944, but the paranormal activity continued unabated. The poltergeist activity simply moved across the road to the nearby Borley Church where strange activity continues to this day. The Borley Rectory is a haunting that has lasted for centuries. Hundreds of credible witnesses have experienced the ghosts and several generations of Rectory occupants documented the paranormal events. The legend of England's most haunted house will continue to the dismay of the critics who have been unable to disprove the extraordinary history of the Borley Rectory.

Toys "R" Us - Sunnyvale, CA

In Sunnyvale, California children are not the only ones visiting the local Toys "R" Us store. Employees have been seeing some very strange things happening inside this store after closing. Toys topple from the their shelves and skateboards roll down aisles clanking aimlessly into the walls. Employees were pelted with flying objects from 20 feet away. Neatly stacked toys that had been set up under lock and key were discovered completely scattered in disarray the following morning. Police alarms are constantly being tripped and there are also creepy stories of the doll that would cry, "mama," over and over again until it would be removed from inside the theft protection box.

The stories have drawn attention and sales for the store, but the employees are spooked. Many quit and most will not work in certain parts of the store at night. The bewildered store management contacted the help of Sylvia Brown, a private psychic counselor, in hopes of getting to the bottom of the haunting. Brown knew exactly which aisles were causing the most problems. She said that the ghost's name was Johnny and he was searching for his love. After some research was done, it was discovered that there was a John Johnson, a circuit preacher who moved to Sunnyvale at the turn of the century, who grew apples on the land where the toy store is now built. John was in love with Elizabeth Murphy, daughter of a prominent rancher, but his love went unrequited and he died unhappy and alone. Despite the efforts of psychics and ghost eliminators, the haunting of the California Toys "R" Us continues.

The Bell House - Robertson County, TN

In the early 1800's, John Bell pioneered his family from North Carolina to Red River in Robertson County, Tennessee. John purchased land, built a log cabin, and quickly gained friends and prominence in the community. One day, in 1817, while walking through his fields, John spotted a strange looking creature. He described it as having a dog's body with a rabbit's head. John shot at the animal, but it disappeared. That night, strange phenomena began occurring in the Bell's cabin. First came a "beating" sound that came from outside of the cabin and continued for a few days, compounding in force with each night. The Bell children began waking up in the middle of the night terrified from hearing gnawing sounds at the foot of their beds and complaining that something was pulling away their covers and pillows as they slept.

John confided in a good friend and neighbor, James Johnson. Mr. and Mrs. Johnson stayed one night at the Bell's cabin. They were barraged the entire night with terrifying sounds and bed covers that would tear away from them and fly across the room. There were also several physical attacks on the Johnson's that included slaps and beatings by unseen forces. Bizarre whispers seemed to come out of thin air.

The family was living in utter terror and when things seemed like they could not get any worse, the strange whispers turned into a relentless female voice that constantly talked to the Bell family and members of the community. The voice spoke to them at night and terrified the family everyday by throwing objects and attacking them. This supernatural presence became known as the Bell Witch.

The sons of John Bell fought under the command of then general, Andrew Jackson. General Jackson had heard about the witch and decided to travel to the Bell cabin to investigate the strange disturbances. As Jackson and his entourage of several soldiers approached the Bell farm in a large wagon, all of the wheels suddenly locked up. Despite attempts, the horses and men could not get the wagon to budge an inch. It is said that Jackson spoke aloud, "this must be the work of the witch." Exactly at that moment, the female's voice spoke back telling Jackson and his men that they could now precede to the house and that she would talk to them again later that night. The wheels on the wagon started turning again.

Later that night, one of Jackson's men, brought because of his occult knowledge, fell under an attack by the unseen forces. The witch's voice taunted the men throughout the night. In the morning, Jackson and his men were seen fleeing the Bell house. Jackson was later quoted saying, "I'd rather fight the entire British army than to deal with the Bell Witch." Andrew Jackson would go on to become the seventh president of the United States of America.

The witch continued to terrorize the Bell family for years. On December 20, 1820, John Bell died. At his bedside, a small vile of a strange liquid was discovered. John Bell Jr. gave some of the liquid to a family cat, which died instantly. The witch spoke up saying that she gave a big dose of that to John last night and that fixed him. John Jr. threw the vile into the fireplace where it shattered causing a blue flame to shoot up the chimney. At John Bell's funeral, the witch reportedly laughed and cackled loudly and sang a song about a bottle of brandy.

After John Bell's death, most of the contact between the witch and the Bell family took place with John Jr. He noted in-depth conversations he had with the witch. He wrote out everything in detailed manuscripts. Their discussions ranged from spiritual topics like the origins of life to the incredible predictions of the Civil War, World War I, the Great Depression, and World War II. When the witch finally said farewell to the Bell family, it vowed to return in 107 years later and visit the Bell descendents. It is believed that in 1935, exactly 107 years after the witch disappeared, she returned as promised and made a new home in a cave on the old Bell property. Since then, there have been strange noises, unexplained voices, and the sounds of children playing inside the abandoned cave. There have also been photographs taken at the site that show a dark figure in the background. After expert review, the negatives of all of the pictures were found to be authentic.

Whaley House - San Diego, CA

Thomas Whaley built the house in 1857, consisting of a living room, kitchen, four bedrooms, a music room, and a courtroom. Several strange and mysterious deaths have occurred in the Whaley house and now many people believe that the ghosts of those people are haunting the house.

One of the ghosts still lingering in the house is Violet Whaley, the daughter of Thomas Whaley. She was supposedly upset over her recent divorce so she moved back home to be close to her family. Nothing she did could relieve her pain and unhappiness. The mysterious details of Violet's suicide have been debated for years. She wrote a suicide note and left it on the back porch, but it was not found until after her death, which was strange considering that her father was on the back porch for the last twenty minutes of Violet's life. Another strange fact was that Violet shot herself in the chest with a .32 revolver, but the authorities never found the gun. Her lonely ghost can still be seen from time to time haunting the house.

Another reported ghost is that of a young neighbor girl who ran over through the Whaley's yard from across the street and accidentally hung herself on a low hanging clothesline. Despite the story, no actual report of the young girl's death can be found in local records.

The murdered soul of a young woman can also be seen haunting the grounds. She was the girlfriend of a man who rented the upstairs living quarters from the Whaley family. One night, during a drunken rage, the man accused her of cheating on him. He chased her from the house and stabbed her to death with a kitchen knife in the middle of the street.

Even Thomas Whaley himself is suspected of still haunting the house that he built. It was said that he would continue to haunt the house until an unpaid county debt of $385 was paid in full to his family. All of these unhappy ghosts supposedly meet in the outside garden everyday.

The Hollywood Roosevelt Hotel - Los Angeles, CA

The Hollywood Roosevelt Hotel was build for the staggering cost of $2.5 million in 1927 and quickly became the essence of excitement, glamour, and elegance that made Hollywood famous. Charles Toberman, who was known as "the father of Hollywood," headed the hotel's construction. Built across the Boulevard from the Chinese Theater, the Roosevelt quickly became the gathering place for Hollywood celebrities and lavish post-premier parties. The first Academy Awards presentation (then called the Merit Awards), was held in the hotel's Blossom Room on May 16, 1929. Hollywood's elite such as Clark Gable, Shirley Temple, and Marilyn Monroe are among a few who stayed at the hotel. By the 1950's, the building had fallen into a steady state of decay. The interior and exterior had become less than glamorous and the Hollywood stars stopped visiting. The cost of repair was greater than the revenue. The Hotel was nearly torn down in the 1980's before the Radisson hotel chain bought it to fully restore it to its former glory.

The ghosts began appearing in December of 1985, two weeks before the historic hotel was scheduled to reopen. The hotel personnel knew something strange was happening right away. The hotel compiled a list of all of the unexplained events that had occurred and passed it out amongst the employees. The list soon became a hot topic and was even passed out to the hotel's guests. The discontented spirit of a man wearing all black was seen in the Blossom Ballroom. As employees approached the stranger, he vanished. There is a spot in the ballroom exactly 30 inches in diameter that is always 10 degrees cooler than the rest of the room.

Another hotel employee was dusting the general manager's office when she discovered a ghost. The employee saw the reflection of a blonde woman standing behind her in the mirror. The woman turned around to say hello to the woman, but she wasn't there. When the employee turned back to double check the mirror, she saw the reflection of the female ghost still standing behind her. It turns out the mirror had once belonged to Marilyn Monroe. The mirror has since been moved out of the manager's office and into the area of the elevator landing.

Around the time same time the upstairs maids were also getting their first introduction to the ghosts. On the 9th floor, a maid felt a cold breeze blow over her. She thought nothing of it because there was still construction work being done to the Hotel and some doors were left open. When she went into room 928, the door suddenly slammed behind her. This startled the maid because the doors are on compression hinges and cannot slam.

The strange events continued after the hotel opened. At first, only public areas and floors 2, 3, and 4 were completed and ready to use. Yet, one night there was a phone call to the front desk from room 1032. The hotel desk responded, but no one was on the line. Room 1032 was not finished and it did not have a phone.

Not long after the hotel was fully opened, guests started complaining about strange noises, people talking loudly in the hallways in the middle of the night, and lights that turned on and off. Security never found anything to be causing the problems and the rooms with the loud noises were always unoccupied.

Other mysterious occurrences included ghosts that moved clipboards and the sound of electric typewriters coming from empty rooms. The room 1221 has a phone that constantly jumps off the hook. Security replaced the phone with a brand new one only to discover the next morning that the phone was back off the hook.

In October of 1989, a television crew was at the hotel to film a Halloween special. They ran into a few problems. First, the lights in the hotel went out and the crew's sound system stopped working. The lights came back on only to go right back out again and this time the crew's camera jammed. When they tried to film Marilyn's mirror, the smoke alarm unexplainably went off.

Later the following year in 1990, the Los Angeles County District Attorney held a dinner dance party at the hotel. After the party was over, one of the guests and the district attorney's wife heard piano music being played. They followed the music into the ballroom and found a man wearing a white suit playing the piano. As they approached, the music stopped and the man vanished.

To this day, the hotel has 4 or 5 different ghostly events happen each month. The Hollywood Roosevelt Hotel seems to be the place for classy ghosts to stay when visiting Los Angeles. Rooms for the living are also available, if you can handle it.

Raynham Hall - Norfolk, England

The Raynham Hall in Norfolk, England is owned by the Townsand family and has stood for almost two hundred years. From the early days of this hall, people have been seeing something that they cannot explain: a strange dark figure floating down the hallways.

The first reported sighting of the brown lady, as the figure is called, occurred near Christmas in 1835 by Colonel Loftus. Loftus was staying at the Hall over the holidays when late one night, while walking back to his room, he saw a strange figure ahead of him. As he approached the figure, it vanished before his eyes. The following week, Loftus saw the ghost again. He described her as a noble woman, wearing a brown satin dress with a face that seemed to glow, eerily highlighting her empty eye sockets. Colonel Loftus told his story, which set off a chain reaction of people coming forward who also claimed to see the ghost. Apparently, the other witnesses had kept silent out of the fear of sounding crazy. Loftus made a sketch of the brown lady. That sketch was made into a painting by an artist and hung in the room that the ghost seemed to frequent.

Another credible sighting of the ghost took place when Caption Fredrick Marryat stayed at the hall. The captain and two other friends were walking down a hallway corridor when they saw the brown lady coming toward them. The men all quickly moved behind a room door and watched the ghost pass by. They said that the ghost was aware of their presence, saying that its head turned to stare the men down with an unearthly phantom glare as it passed. Captain Marryat jumped out from behind the door with his pistol drawn and fired one shot directly into the back of the ghost's head. The brown lady vanished.

Many years later on September 19, 1936, two photographers from Country Lake Magazine managed to take a photograph of the brown lady completely by accident. The photographers were at the hall to shoot pictures of the staircase for the cover of their magazine. While they were setting up, one of the men saw the ghost gliding down the steps of the staircase. He screamed out for the other to take the picture. The photographer took the picture and what came out is one of the most amazing ghost photographs ever taken. It showed a dark hooded figure slowing descending the staircase. The photograph came under heavy attack by skeptic's who claimed the photo had to be a fraud, but after professional examination, there was no trace that the picture had ever been tampered with or altered. By all accounts, the brown lady photograph is valid. The photograph of the brown lady still stands today as possibly the best ghost photo ever taken.

One of the strangest aspects of the Raynham Hall ghost is her identity. No one knows who the brown lady is or why she haunts the hall. She was seen in the early days of the hall and yet, no deaths had occurred at the hall. Her identity and origins remain a mystery.

The Myrtles Plantation - St. Francisville, LA

The Myrtles Plantation is located about seventy miles north of New Orleans, Louisiana. The Plantation has been featured in several magazines and television programs because of its incredible architecture. The U.S. Tourist Bureau also lists the plantation as an authentic American haunted house.

General David Bradford built the Myrtles Plantation in the late 18th century. Bradford acquired the land through the Spanish Land Grant. Then, he set forth to build his dream home. He picked the highest spot of land to protect the house from the flooding rains. The land where Bradford selected to build was high for a reason. Local Indian tribes had used the area as a sacred burial ground. Despite objections to digging up Indian ground, the General went on with his project. On the orders of General Bradford, all of the Indian bones found while digging the foundation were piled up and burned.

Desecrating the Indian holy ground was said to have supernatural consequences, but the General said the only supernatural thing that he ever witnessed was the occasional phantom sighting of a naked Indian girl walking across the small pond behind the house. He said that the ghost was almost completely transparent and always weeping. General Bradford lived the rest of his life at the Plantation and died of natural causes.

After the General's death, the house was sold to Sarah Mathilda Bradford Woodruff, the General's daughter, and her husband, Judge Clarke Woodruff. It was not long until the Judge had chosen a slave mistress by the name of Chloe. As legend tells, one afternoon Chloe was caught listening to one of the Judges private business deals and, as punishment, the Judge had her left ear cut off.

For the remainder of her life Chloe wore a green turban to hide the disfigurement. In a show of good faith and perhaps to secure her place in the house again, Chloe offered to bake a cake for the family. The Judge accepted her offer unaware that Chloe had a surprise planned. She was baking the cake with oleander flower, a poison.

It was believed that Chloe's plan was to put just enough poison in the cake to make the family sick. Then, she would come into the house and nurse the family back to full health. However, she misjudged the amount of poison. Sarah and her two daughters died as a result. The Judge was lucky enough not to eat the cake.

When the Judge discovered what happened, he was enraged. Chloe ran away fearing for her life. She fled to her family's cabin and begged them for help, but her family would not help. Instead, Chloe's family dragged her to a large oak tree and hung her in the desperate hope that her punishment would bring leniency on the rest of the family.

Judge Woodruff ordered that her dead body be left hanging from the oak tree for several days. When she was finally cut down, the Judge refused to let her be buried and ordered that her lifeless body be thrown into the Mississippi River. After the terrible event, Judge Woodruff sold the Plantation and moved to New Orleans.

Since Chloe's death, witnesses have reported seeing her ghost still roaming the Plantation in the middle of the night. A baby's cry can be heard when she is seen. The baby is believed to be either one of the Bradford children that Chloe murdered or possibly a baby that Chloe was carrying at the time she was killed.

Other strange events at the Myrtles Plantation include bizarre pools of blood forming on the ground, the ghosts of two little girls peeking through windows, and a phantom confederate soldier who keeps watch over the Plantation as he marches back and forth across the porch. A strange apparition of an old man has been seen manifesting from time to time at the front gate warning people away from the house. There is also the strange recurring ghost sighting of a slave voodoo priestess chanting over the apparition of a young girl.

Phantom Ships

The Flying Dutchman

The Flying Dutchman is probably the best known of all the phantom ships. While many of the stories of the fate of the Flying Dutchman are largely sea tales, they are based on facts. The Flying Dutchman was a real ship Captained by Hendrick Vanderdecken. It set sail from Amsterdam on its way to Batavia, a port in Dutch East India, in 1680. After its departure from port, the Flying Dutchman was never seen again. According to the popular legend, Vanderdecken's ship encountered a severe storm as it was rounding the Cape of Good Hope. Vanderdecken ignored the dangers of the storm, which was thought by the crew to be a warning from God. He ordered the crew to press on through the storm and taunted the men with cowardly remarks. Vanderdecken stood on the deck and yelled out to God, daring Him to sink the ship.

As the storm beat down on the Flying Dutchman, a dark apparition suddenly appeared on the deck. Vanderdecken removed his pistol and ordered the spirit to leave his ship. The tempest increased and the ship floundered, sending all aboard to their deaths. As punishment, Vanderdecken and his ship were doomed to sail the waters near the Cape for eternity.

The first sighting of the Flying Dutchman came in 1835, over one hundred and fifty years after its disappearance. The captain and crew of a British ship recorded that they saw the phantom ship approaching in the shroud of a terrible storm. It came so close that the British crew feared the two ships might collide, but then the ghost ship suddenly vanished. The ship was the Flying Dutchman.

The next sighting came from the H.M.S. Bacchante in 1881. It was again seen in 1939, by dozens of sunbathers off the coast of South Africa. The last know sighting was in 1942, off the coast of Cape Town. Witnesses saw the Flying Dutchman sail into Table Bay only to vanish before their eyes.

The Griffon

At the time the Griffon was built in the seventeenth century, it was the largest ship to sail the Great Lakes. After her maiden voyage, the Griffon set sail with full cargo and was expected to return to the harbors in Niagara on September 18, 1679. The Griffon never arrived. To this day, no one knows what fate befell the doomed ship or its crew. Legend tells that the Griffon sailed through a crack in the ice and vanished from reality. In 1955, wreckage resembling the Griffon was discovered off Bruce Peninsula in Lake Huron, but the true identity of the found ship remains unidentified. On dark and foggy nights, the phantom Griffon can be seen floating aimlessly throughout the Great Lakes.

Mary Celeste

The Mary Celeste story is an intriguing tale. On December 3, 1872, the crew of the Dei Gratia, while sailing from New York to Gibraltar, discovered the unmanned Mary Celeste drifting about 600 miles west of Portugal. The ship was intact and in perfect sailing condition. The sails were set, its cargo of 1,700 barrels of commercial alcohol were untouched, and breakfast meals looked as though they had been abandoned in the middle of being eaten. All of the crew's belongings remained onboard. The only things missing from the ship besides the captain, Benjamin S. Briggs, his wife, daughter, and the ship's crew of seven, were the ship's chronometer, the sextant (used for guidance and direction), and the cargo documents. There were no signs of a struggle, foul play, piracy, or a violent storm. The last ships log was made on November 24, and made no indications of problems or trouble. The Mary Celeste was abandoned for almost two weeks, yet someone or something had to be working the controls of the ship in order to end up where the Dei Gratia found it. Debate exists over what happened on board the Mary Celeste. The fate of her Captain, his family, and the crew is unknown.

The Queen Mary

This ship is rumored to be home to many different ghosts, from unexplained knockings and dark figures, to children's footprints and the appearance of a lady in white. It all began during World War II when the Queen Mary accidentally collided with a military ship. The Queen Mary was fine, but the military ship was cut in half and sank fast. Hundreds of soldiers were killed. When the Queen Mary returned to port for repairs, it was discovered that a man from the other ship had been thrown through a hole torn in the hull above the water line. He had been alive after the accident, but died of exposure during the trip. Many technicians and workers will not go into that area of the ship by themselves at night.

In another area of the ship a young man, only 17 years old, was crushed to death by a watertight door in 1966 during a routine drill. Since then, people have reported hearing strange knocking sounds on the pipes and unexplained bright lights where the boy was killed.

Even the ship's pool is haunted. The ghosts of two children, one boy and one girl, have been seen playing. The phantom girl asks people for her mother or a baby doll. Not much is known about the phantom children, but there is a story that the girl is allegedly a young girl that fell down some stairs and broke her neck.

Ship stowaways would die in engine room 2 every time the ship would fire up the boilers to leave port. Moans from the phantom stowaways can be heard echoing deep in the bows of the ship. Other ghost sightings include a mysterious woman in white who walks the deck. She can be seen until blocked from view by a pillar where she mysteriously vanishes. A ghostly elderly couple has been seen walking the hall to either side of the main entry to the first class rooms. It is surprising that this ship can hold any living passengers. It seems to be packed full with ghosts!

Poltergeists

The Smurl Poltergeist

From 1985 to 1987 the home of Jack and Janet Smurl was the scene of a terrifying poltergeist. The horrible events that took place in the Smurl home could have come straight out of a horror movie. It was believed that the supernatural phenomenon was the work of an evil spirit or demon. Famous demonologists, Ed and Lorraine Warren, investigated the case and the house underwent four separate exorcisms by the Catholic Diocese.

The Smurls were practicing Catholics with strong religious beliefs. At the time, they were living in a duplex with Jack's parents because a hurricane and massive flooding had forced them from their own home. They had stayed in the house for 18 peaceful months before the strange phenomena began to occur. The first signs of poltergeist activity started small with a stain on the new carpet that continued to reappear after it was scrubbed away. Soon after, the television set exploded in flames and the water pipes began to leak even after they were soldered several different times. An odd sour smell filled the home. New bathroom fixtures were found scratched to pieces as if a wild animal had violently clawed them. Not long after that Dawn, the eldest daughter, started seeing ghostly figures floating around her bedroom at night.

Soon the house was in chaos with what the family now thought was a haunting. Toilets were flushing with no one in the bathroom. Radios played when they were not plugged in. Porch chairs were found rocking with no one sitting in them and unexplained footsteps were heard walking up and down the steps at night. These circumstances were nothing more than annoying until later that year when the disturbances took a turn for the worse becoming terrifyingly violent. It started with the house turning ice cold. Mysterious voices yelled out obscene and abusive language. Then, a dark and sinister apparition appeared to the family.

The first life-threatening incident took place when a heavy light fixture somehow fell over and landed on Shannon Smurl, almost killing her. Loud rapping noises filled the walls. The family's dog, a German Shepard, was repeatedly levitated and thrown across the room. Snake-like hissing sounds crept into bedrooms and unexplained screams echoed in the house.

The first physical attack came just after a moment of intimacy between Jack and Janet Smurl. Janet was violently pulled from the bed by an unseen force while Jack remained paralyzed in the bed gagging. In a separate room, Shannon was also thrown from her bed. This was only the beginning of the horror.

Desperate needs call for desperate measures. In January of 1986, the Smurls learned about the professional demonologists, the Warrens. The Smurls were skeptical, but felt that they had nothing to lose. They contacted the Warrens who arrived with Rosemary Frueh, a registered nurse and psychic. After extensive questioning and touring of the Smurl home, the team was able to detect four different supernatural entities inside the home. Three of these entities were minor and harmless, but the Warrens claimed that the fourth spirit was a demon.

The first attempts by the Warrens to get the demon to expose itself resulted in mirrors shaking and dresser drawers shooting open. The Warrens played religious music throughout the house, spread holy water, and prayed. Despite these efforts, the poltergeist activity continued and the words, "You filthy bastards. Get out of this house," were scrolled on a wall, allegedly by the demon.

The attempts to communicate with the demon only seemed to enrage it. One night Jack claims to have been raped by the demon posing as an old woman. He said that her eyes were glowing red and her gums were green. Later, Janet was also sexually attacked by the demon while pig noises squealed inside the walls. The attacks were not left only to the Smurls. Ed Warren fell victim to a violent attack. Unseen hands choked Ed while pushing him toward the stairs.

The Roman Catholic Diocese of Scranton was contacted about performing an exorcism. After the contact, there were several instances were Janet thought that she was getting help from a local priest only to later discover that it was the demon in disguise.

The violent episodes continued to escalate. Dawn Smurl was attacked and almost raped by the demon. Things in the house were out of hand. Everyone involved was being viciously scratched, bitten, and attacked on a regular basis. Ed Warren called the events unfolding a result of a serious demon infestation. The Smurls attempted to leave on several occasions, but the poltergeist would only follow them, even to their work places. The Catholic Church finally stepped in and preformed four exorcisms. The poltergeist activity and violent attacks stopped.

The Enfield Poltergeist

In 1977, a poltergeist flared up in Enfield in North London. On a late night in August, Janet Harper, then 11 years old, and her brother Pete, then 10, began complaining that their beds were, "jolting up and down and going all funny." When their mother would come into the room, the beds had stopped moving. She suspected that the children were faking the entire thing as a joke.

It was not long before strange shuffling noises and loud knocking sounds on the walls could be heard daily throughout the home. When Mrs. Harper saw a heavy chest slide across the floor under its own control, she took the children from the house to the neighbors. The neighbors came over to the house and thoroughly searched it. They could not find anyone else inside the house.

The local police were called in to investigate. They were also unable to find anyone in the house or any cause for the strange knocking sounds that they were hearing in the home. During the police search, an officer saw a chair slide across the floor all by itself. It was enough to spook the officer and the event was written up in the final report.

In the days that followed, several people visiting the house witnessed unexplainable events. The poltergeist was gaining energy. Toy Lego bricks and small marbles were randomly thrown. Objects in the house were found hot to the touch.

Maurice Grosse from the Society for Psychical Research was called to investigate. Maurice claimed that during his investigation, unseen hands threw marbles and doors would open and close without assistance.

Soon, writer Guy Lyon Playfair joined Maurice to help study the case. By this time, the strange knocking sounds had become a nightly occurrence. Furniture slid in front of people. Dresser drawers shot out. Bedclothes were pulled off. Objects levitated and flew across rooms. Mysterious puddles of water were discovered on the floors and unexplained fires would start up then abruptly extinguish themselves.

When the poltergeist was at its highest level, the case took a turn for the disturbing. Speaking through 11-year-old Janet, in a deep manly voice, a ghost began communicating. Grosse and Playfair recorded the little girl's possession on both audiotape and film. The spirit revealed that his name was Bill and that he had died in that house. Photographs were taken in the house allegedly showing Janet levitating off of the bed.

Skeptics point out that the Enfield Poltergeist activity always disappears when Janet was watched closely. When she was taken away to the hospital for testing, the poltergeist also ceased. They believe that Janet was faking the possession. They claim that the picture of the young girl levitating is actually Janet jumping off of the bed. The skeptical conclusion to this case was that a little girl looking for some attention was faking the poltergeist activity.

Still, others pointed to the evidence of the police officers that heard the knocking sounds and saw furniture move and the other witnesses that were hit by flying objects when Janet was not even inside the house. They maintain that this 11-year-old girl could not fake such an elaborate supernatural hoax with independent investigators inside the house. However you choose to judge the events that occurred in the Enfield Poltergeist, it remains one of the best cases in recent times.

Haunted Cemeteries

Bachelor's Grove Cemetery - Near Chicago, IL

Bachelor's Grove is considered by many visitors to be one of the most haunted cemeteries in the Chicago area and possibly, the world. The cemetery was founded in 1844 when one of the local settlers was buried in the grove where the families picnicked and fished at the nearby pond. The cemetery was completely abandoned in the 1960's. Since then, vandals have destroyed and carried off most of the tombstones, leaving only a few on the eastern half. The fences are destroyed and trash is scattered throughout the cemetery. Hundreds of people have visited this cemetery and there are hundreds of ghost stories associated with it.

There are rumors that in the late 1920's and 30's, the mafia dumped its victims in the grove. They used the grove because of its remote location and close proximity to Chicago. Visitors have seen a black phantom car driving fast and weaving down the small road. Several unsuspecting drivers have told stories of a phantom automobile that crashes into the side of their cars at the turnpike exit before racing away into the darkness. When the driver gets out to investigate the damage, there is not a scratch on the vehicle.

There are other instances where the phantom car collides head-on with oncoming vehicles. The terrified victims close their eyes and scream only to discover that the phantom car passes right through them before vanishing. The car has chased people off the road and tried to run down visitors walking on the path.

Legend is that the phantom car is actually the same car that the mobsters used to dump dead bodies at the grove. Many believe that the gangster is cursed to continue his route of death throughout eternity. Others believe that that the gangster died in an automobile accident or was murdered on that road.

Another unusual apparition in the grove is an old looking man, dressed in a long black trench coat. Many visitors who have seen this apparition believe it to be a ghoul or the walking dead. Witnesses see the man when they are leaving the cemetery. The man has also been seen on the road by cars traveling to the cemetery. No one knows the man's exact identity, but one possible suspect is the old groundskeeper who killed his entire family with an ax before hanging himself on the roadside. To support this story, there is the ghost of a man sometimes seen hanging from a tree at the grove.

One of the most peculiar and interesting characteristics of Bachelor's Grove cemetery is the phantom house. Visitors have seen a floating two-story Victorian style house, complete with a front porch, a swing, and drapes. When visitors approach the house, it vanishes. Different eyewitnesses have drawn pictures of the floating house. Those pictures have matched exactly with other witness drawings. The only detail that varies is the location, which seems to change from sighting to sighting.

During the 1970's, the cemetery was taken over by groups of satanic worshipers who desecrated the cemetery. Tombstones were vandalized, visitors were robbed, and bodies were unearthed. The rumor is that men wearing full black robes conducted satanic rituals in the cemetery at night. Since then, visitors have reported seeing phantom black "monk" apparitions that many believe are the ghosts of the devil worshipers continuing their unholy rituals.

There is also a tragic story of a farmer and his horse. The legend is that a farmer was working in the nearby field with this horse plow when something spooked the horse. The horse bucked wildly and ran out of control. The farmer became twisted in the reins and was thrown to the ground knocking him out cold. The horse continued to run and pulled the plow and the unconscious farmer into the pond where they both drowned. Visitors have seen a phantom horse splashing in the nearby pond and a ghostly farmer working in the field. There is also a strange blue light that floats over the pond before disappearing.

And, of course, no haunted cemetery would be complete without a White Lady ghost. This female ghost appears frequently and some visitors have allegedly photographed her standing sadly in the cemetery. The White Lady seems to be searching for something, possibly a lost child, amongst the graves. There have been ghostly blue lights and strange round orbs hovering in the cemetery at the time the White Lady appears. She manifests as a semi-transparent figure that seems to glide smoothly over the ground. Many psychics brought to the cemetery feel intense sadness and depression emanating from the lost spirit of a young woman.

The evidence needed to verify the Bachelor Grove legends are impossible to acquire. Records at the time were poorly kept and many of these small towns turned into ghost towns almost overnight. The truth of Bachelor's Grove may never be known, but the visitors who venture to the cemetery searching for paranormal activity are rarely disappointed. Unlike many conventional haunts, Bachelor's Grove is a unique haunting with extraordinary ghosts, putting it into a class all its own.

Stull Cemetery - Stull, KS - The Gateway to Hell

If most people were asked where the home of evil could be found, they probably would not guess Kansas, but some believe that's exactly where true evil is most likely to be found. Ten miles west of Lawrence, Kansas, in the Northeast part of the state, is the sleepy town of Stull, named after its original postmaster Silvester Stull, born in 1862. There are only a handful of houses left today inside the city limits. On the edge of the town is Stull cemetery, the black heart of all the trouble.

At first glance, Stull cemetery appears to be an average sight at best. There are less than a hundred tombstones and a burned out church sitting peacefully on a well-kept hillside. Nothing about the cemetery looks strange or abnormal, but don't try to visit. The local sheriff patrols regularly. There are no trespassing signs clearly posted. If trespassers are caught inside the cemetery grounds, at any time of the day or night, they are arrested on the spot and taken to jail to await trial, charged with criminal trespassing. The punishment seems harsh, but apparently necessary to keep away vandals and the hordes of demon hunters that flock to Stull cemetery by the hundreds every year.

Time Magazine asked Pope John Paul II why he ordered his plane to fly around Kansas on his way to a 1995 speaking engagement in Colorado. He answered, because he didn't want to fly over the, "unholy ground." One resident of Stull recently quoted by a local newspaper said, "I would never go to Stull cemetery and it's not the sheriff that scares me."

All the hype could revolve around the fact that Stull shares the Topeka zip code prefix, 666. Or, maybe it's the fact that the main road through Stull was called Devils Lane until its name change in 1905. There are numerous legends surrounding this small town and its mysterious cemetery.

The legends surrounding Stull Cemetery have been floating around for over 100 years. The stories were passed down from generation to generation through local Stull families. Students who were told the Stull cemetery folklore by their grandparents, put the stories into a University of Kansas newspaper article back in 1974. Since then, hundreds of people have traveled long pilgrimages from all over the world for a chance to witness the strange phenomenon of Stull cemetery.

Following the student article, haunted reference guides and occult books listed Stull cemetery as one of the few places on earth where Satan allegedly manifests from a supernatural gateway. If the legends are true, one of the seven gateways to Hell opens up somewhere on the cemetery grounds allowing the Devil to step through into our world.

The rumor is Satan comes to the cemetery to visit the gravesite of his unholy son who was buried within the grounds. This unnatural phenomenon only happens twice a year, once on the Spring Equinox and again exactly at the stroke of midnight on Halloween night. The exact dates have caused confusion and debate among visitors. Many visitors journey to Stull cemetery expecting to meet Satan October 31st. While October 31st is the calendar date for the Halloween holiday, the actual pagan Halloween holiday takes place on the first full moon in the month of October.

The exact location of the gateway to Hell remains unknown. The fire-damaged church, built in 1867, located on the top of the cemetery's hill, seems to be the center of the controversy. It's thought by many to be the location of the gateway. The church was never restored after a mysterious fire swept through it back in the early 1900's leaving only the four walls. Rumor is that the fire was either a direct result of engulfing flames exiting from the open gateway or that the deeply religious community destroyed the church attempting to hide or destroy the secret gateway. Despite the fact that the church roof is completely burned away, the legend is that no rain will fall inside the church. The rain slides away from the church as if there were an invisible roof above the frame.

Another secret to the Stull mystery revolves around a pine tree planted about the same time that the church was built. Many years later it was rumored that the tree was used to hang witches who came to the cemetery to celebrate the Equinox. A local Stull man was also reported missing only to be later discovered hanging from the tree with no explanation for his death. The gigantic tree continued to grow until it was so large that its roots split a tombstone next to it. This was considered a bad omen.

More recently, modern witches began traveling back to the tree that they now considered sacred to worship and to pay tribute to the witches hung from the tree. In 1998, the tree was more than 150 years old. Two days before Halloween, the caretakers chopped down the tree and removed it.

When asked why the tree was removed, the caretakers said that it was because the tree had died. However, individuals at the scene took pictures and posted them on the Internet. The pictures clearly show that the tree was healthy and alive at the time the tree was being chopped down, contradicting the caretaker's reports. Many also speculate if the trees removal only two days before Halloween was mere coincidence.

If that were the end of the Stull cemetery legends it would be a creepy place, but there are more stories about this small cemetery that the people in Stull don't want you to know. Visitors to the cemetery have reportedly had violent run-ins with locals who forced them off the road with pickup trucks. Stull cemetery websites have received hate mail and even death threats from anonymous individuals who want the websites to be taken down. Despite the harassment, the legends of Stull cemetery persist.

Other strange Stull legends include a werewolf who visits the cemetery to make deals with the Devil, demons, and other evil creatures that come and go from the gateway; occultists performing strange satanic rituals, witches holding black mass, and phantom specters swinging from nooses at the pine tree. The church remains glowing red on certain nights and sometimes a strange set of stair steps near the church that lead down into the ground appears. These steps to nowhere are also another possible location of the gateway to Hell. The legend is that a person can walk down these steps and come back up two weeks later, even though it has only seemed like seconds have passed.

To add even more fuel to the fire, on Halloween night 1999, news reporters from The Lawrence Journal World and Sunflower Cable station Channel 6 News were at the cemetery. The local sheriff was on patrol, but didn't ask the news crews to leave. At 11:30 PM (perfect timing), thirty minutes from the time that the gateway to Hell was scheduled to open, an unknown representative for the cemetery owners appeared from the darkness and ordered everyone off of the property. With the sheriff present, the news crews left peacefully.

The cemetery caretakers claim that they don't want the attention or media coverage because it attracts vandals to the cemetery. If the caretakers didn't want people coming to the cemetery to find Satan, then they should have let the news teams film at midnight. Nothing would have discouraged potential visitors more than seeing video footage of nothing happening on Halloween night.

The endless legends of Stull cemetery continue to grow with each passing year. Visitors dare to continue traveling to the off limits cemetery at their own risk, endeavoring to find answers to this old puzzle, but no one may ever know the real truth. Stull is a town that protects its secrets.

"Forty miles west of Kansas City, down a country road like a lonely soul, I see Sharon and I see Jack. It's me and Roman dressed in black. Tell my bride to bury me in Stull...Don't be afraid. Don't be afraid. It's great." - *Song lyrics of Stull Part 1 by Urge Overkill.*

Resurrection Cemetery - Chicago, IL

The story of Resurrection Mary, the vanishing hitchhiker, has to be Chicago's most famous ghost story. The ghost is believed by some to be Mary Bregovy, a young girl who died on March 10, 1934. The legend says that she was dancing at the now closed O'Henry Ballroom when she got into a fight with her boyfriend. She stormed out of the ballroom and started to hitchhike back home. Somewhere between Willowbrook and the main gates of Resurrection Cemetery, Mary was struck and killed by a hit and run driver. Soon afterwards, people began seeing a beautiful young blonde haired girl, wearing a long white dress, hitchhiking along Archer Avenue near the cemetery.

The first person to come forward with a story about picking up Mary was Jerry Palus. He said that he picked up a girl at Liberty Grove and they danced the entire night. She was incredibly beautiful. The only thing that seemed strange to him was that the girl was ice cold to the touch.

After dancing, she asked Jerry for a ride home, which was over in the Bridgeport area. She asked if they could take an out of the way route home past Resurrection Cemetery. Jerry drove the way she wanted to go, but as they got closer to the cemetery Mary began acting strange. She told Jerry to pull the car off the road. He stopped the car and Mary bolted running off toward the cemetery gates. Jerry watched her running, but before she made it to the gate she vanished into thin air right before this eyes.

Confused and frightened, Jerry continued to drive to Mary's home thinking that it was a practical joke. He knocked on the door and was greeted by an older woman who told him that her daughter was dead. Jerry saw a picture of the dead girl on the stand. It was the same girl that he had danced with that night.

The story could have ended there been written off as another phantom hitchhiker urban legend, but this ghost story did not end. People continued to see a beautiful hitchhiker at the side of the road and sometimes dancing around trees and tombstones inside the cemetery.

In 1979, a cab driver coming back from dropping off a fare spotted a girl at the side of the road. The driver described her as nice looking blonde girl, around 21 years old, wearing a fancy white dress. She had no coat despite the fact that it was snowy and very cold. She looked right at the cab. The driver stopped, thinking that she was having car problems.

The girl jumped right into the front seat and the cab driver headed up Archer Avenue. He said that the girl seemed funny, like she'd had a couple of drinks. She would only nod her head when he asked if they were going the right direction. The only thing that she said was, "the snow came early this year." The driver said it was like her mind was a million miles away.

As the cab drove further down Archer, the girl started to jump around in her seat. Then, she suddenly yelled out, "Here, Here!" The cab drive hit the brakes and stopped. The girl pointed across the road and said, "There!" The driver turned to look for a second and when he turned back the girl was gone. The cab driver swears that he only looked away for a split second and that the cab door never opened.

There is another Resurrection Mary story recorded by the Justice Police Department. The police department received a phone call one evening from a man who said that he had just driven past the main gates of Resurrection Cemetery and saw a girl that had been apparently locked inside after dark. At 10:30 PM, Sergeant Pat Homa arrived at the scene. He searched for the girl with a spotlight and loudspeaker. He found no one. However, he did find that two of the bars on the main gate had been bent apart. After closer examination, it was discovered that small handprints and skin textures were imbedded into the metal. It was a feat that amazed and bewildered metallurgists who studied the bars.

Unlike typical phantom hitchhikers that are usually only seen by male drivers, numerous female passersby have also seen Resurrection Mary. Countless drivers with passengers have spotted this lonely apparition standing at the side of the road only to see her ghostly disappearance as they stop to help.

Haunted Cities

Athens, Ohio

Located on the banks of the Hocking River in Southeast Ohio, Athens is a place that has been shrouded in mystery since Native American Indians discovered strange stone altars on nearby Mt. Nebo. The Shawnee tribes considered the stone altars magical and the land around them holy ground. They refused to hunt in the area and preformed seasonal rituals there drawing from the earth's natural energy forces.

When the early Europeans began arriving, they also found the region to be very mystical. Before long, thousands of spiritualists were making long pilgrimages to the area. Soon after, in 1804, the city of Athens was founded. The ghostly legends of Athens focus on five old surrounding cemeteries that were deliberately built by the settlers to form a pentagram. Athens falls directly in the center of the pentagram.

Cemetery Pentagram:

There are five major cemeteries, (Simms, Hannin, Cuckler, Higgins, and Zion), that surround Athens. When plotted on a map, they form the shape of a pentagram. The pentagram is a spiritualist symbol used to draw supernatural energy and protection. This pentagram is not the cause of the unusual amount of paranormal activity, but more of a focal lens to control the supernatural energy and to create a safety zone against evil powers that might be drawn to the area.

Visitors to these cemeteries have told many strange ghost stories. Soldiers of the Revolutionary War, the War of 1812, and the Civil War have been seen wondering around the tombstones. Phantom corpses swing from an old hanging tree. Huge cemetery gates mysteriously unlock. Athens residences in the ridges area see the ghosts of people buried in the cemeteries.

The Roberts and Simms families were both cursed for all eternity. Mary Roberts, a known witch, is buried near Magistrate John Simms.   Mary Roberts was cursed for being a witch and Judge Simms was cursed for being the town local magistrate and executioner. The ghosts of each have been seen inside Simms
. There have even been reports of spirits following visitors after they left the cemetery. Restless spirits haunt all five of the main cemeteries.

Ohio University- Athens, OH:

Ohio University is the oldest public institution of higher learning in the state of Ohio and the first in the Northwest Territory. Athens is a very small Ohio town. The tiny population is completely dwarfed by the nearly twenty thousand OU college students. The students are known for throwing one of the nation's largest Halloween parties annually and also host ghost tours. Ohio University is a large part of the town and at the center of the cemetery pentagram. It is no an accident that many of the paranormal events happen on the University's campus.

The AOPi Sorority house, located at 24 E. Washington Street, formally known as the Zeta Tau Alpha House, is still occupied by the ghost of a slave named Nicodemus. The house is the oldest home in Athens and it was used in the Civil War as a stop on the Underground Railroad.

When the house was raided, Nicodemus fled into the basement attempting to escape through a secret tunnel, but he was shot and killed. Each school year new sorority girls befriend the ghost hoping that he will not scare them. They leave notes, light candles, and whisper good night to Nicodemus. The ghost of Nicodemus can be heard scratching and whining behind the wall that hides the secret escape tunnel.

Girls have experienced doors locking and unlocking by themselves, objects disappearing, and loud creaking noises in the living room and on the staircase. The sorority girls have even reported seeing a man in ragged clothing that vanishes before their eyes, allegedly the tormented soul of Nicodemus.

Wilson Hall is another OU building filled with unexplainable phenomena. Wilson Hall is built directly overtop of a graveyard used by the Athens State Hospital, later named the Athens Mental Health and Retardation Center, which old county records confirm was built in 1874. It is also in the exact center of the cemetery pentagram formation.

After a mysterious student death in the 1970's, in room 428, students started to report hearing odd noises, (mysterious footsteps and what sounds like marbles dropping to the floor), along with electric disturbances, and doors opening and closing without explanation. Terrified students would see ghostly apparitions plunging from windows as if they were reenacting a suicide. Objects would fly across rooms and violently smash into walls. The disturbances got so bad that the university closed off room 428. To this day room 428 is sealed off from the students.

Bryan Hall is the oldest hall on the OU campus and one of the most haunted. The creepy attic seems to be the focus of most of the paranormal activity. In the darkness of the attic, storage boxes move out to block off walkways. Ghostly footsteps follow closely behind terrified visitors. Mysterious, freezing cold breezes flow through the room. The words, "Flick Lives '79" are scrolled across the attic wall. Many people believe Flick to be the ghost, and a former student, who committed suicide by hanging himself in room 413.

Students have reported hearing footsteps in empty hallways, lights that turned off and on, and ghosts that drink from water fountains. There is also the strange story of a female student who met a man and invited him to explore the attic with her. They went up into the attic and all the way to the top of the bell tower where they began to kiss. The girl turned her back to the man for a second and when she turned back around, the man had vanished into thin air.

Apparitions and paranormal activities have been reported in almost all of the dormitories associated with Athens, Ohio University, including Jefferson Hall, Washington Hall, Bush Hall, Shively Hall, Crawford Font Four Freshman Halls, and Cutler Hall.

The Ridges:

Possibly the most famous Athens ghost tale comes from the old Athens County Mental Hospital. This hospital of misery was virtually a prison for the patients who were tortured everyday with inhuman treatments. Margaret Schilling, or Marge, was one of the former asylum's residents. She stayed in the open ward because she was not a troublesome patient. Marge was given special privileges and freedoms that other patients did not get. She was free to leave the hospital on the condition that she returned by 8pm. She was also free to wonder the hospital unattended.

It seems that one day, Marge wandered into a wing of the hospital known as Ward N. 20, which was rarely used. The doors closed behind her and when Marge tried to leave, she discovered that the doors had locked. There was a three-day search for Marge, but no one found her until six weeks later. An autopsy discovered that she had died of starvation in Ward N. 20 about four to five weeks before her body was discovered.

The strange part of the story is the mysterious stain that was left behind after her body was removed from the ward. The stain is very detailed, including the imprint of Marge's hairstyle and the wrinkles of her clothes. Despite all attempts to clean the stain from the floor, the stain will simply reappear a few days later.

Ohio University now owns the building and the grounds. No employees are allowed to discuss Margaret Schilling, Ward N. 20, or the mysterious stain on the floor. There have been reports of strange lights appearing in the Ward N. 20 section of the building and the shadowy figure of a female patient gazing out of the windows. It's believed that Marge's ghost is still trapped in the ward and that the stain will remain until her tormented soul can find a way out.

Athens Cults:

It is believed that the land's unique geography created natural psychic energies. It is unknown who built the stone altars on Mt Nebo, but it is obvious that they were used in holy ceremonies or magical practices. The Shawnee Indian tribes practiced mystical rituals at the stones and when the European spiritualists arrived, they continued the pattern of magical practices. It is not known what makes the region so special, but many believe that the area is filled with supernatural energies that can be harnessed and controlled. During the 1960's and 70's, pagan cults flocked to Athens. Local farm animals began turning up dead with their heads and genitalia cut off. Animals were bled to death and mutilated. The cults activities and mutilations decreased in the 1980's and are almost nonexistent today. Athens history of magic and mysticism keeps the supernatural legends alive.

Supernatural Events:

There are many mysterious legends attached to Athens. There is a concrete angel statue in the local cemetery that sheds real tears. Many people have sighted a headless conductor carrying a lantern in the Moonville tunnel, which is near Lake Hope. There are phantom apparitions seen by OU students floating across the campus grounds from their dorm room windows. A strange woman in white appears in the window of her downtown home where she refuses to leave. There is a mischievous ghost of a man who haunts the Memorial Auditorium, appearing in dressing rooms, turning off lights, and pulling out electric cables. The Auditorium also has a female ghost who died falling from the balcony and the ghost of a little girl in the basement that had fallen into a well and died. These ghost stories are a few that make the town of Athens, Ohio one of the world's most haunted cities.

Gettysburg, PA

The most important battle of the Civil War was fought in the small farming community of Gettysburg, PA (population 2,400). The Northern Union and Southern Confederate armies massed together by the thousands and created a Hell on earth for three straight days. The Confederate soldiers, led by General Robert E. Lee, had pushed deep into Northern territory, capturing every Union City along the path. The two great armies had been playing a strategic game of cat and mouse across the treacherous Pennsylvania landscape for months when they met by accident in Gettysburg on July 1, 1863.

No one could have imagined that the three days that followed would forever change the course of American history. The boasting Southern Army saw this battle as another small skirmish on the way to total conquest. They expected to win Gettysburg easily. They had beaten the Union forces across the country, winning every major battle. They were counting down the days until complete victory would be in Southern hands.

The Union troops were desperate for a victory and they knew the importance of this battle. In essence, it was their last stand. A loss at Gettysburg would seal their fate. Determined to not let the Confederates have an early advantage, the Union soldiers pressed forward on the morning of July 1st and attacked the approaching Confederate soldiers along the Chambersburg Road. Outnumbered and flanked by the enemy, the overwhelmed Union soldiers were forced to retreat back to Cemetery Ridge, overlooking the town of Gettysburg, to watch the Confederate Army march into Gettysburg.

Silent meadows and peaceful farmland surrounding Gettysburg roared with the deafening noise of cannon fire, shouting soldiers, and howling of the wounded. Thick, red blood quickly blanketed over the green foliage of the countryside. The small streams ran blood red. Disoriented soldiers and horses slid and fell on the slippery blood soaked ground. Large military regiments gathered in open fields and skirmished back and forth, while Northern and Confederate flags waved around them.

Confederate soldiers quickly took strategic positions inside the homes and buildings of Gettysburg. Meanwhile, the innocent townspeople stayed below in their cellars, not knowing how long this battle would last. Neither side was prepared for a vicious confrontation of this size. Inadequate food supplies ran low fast. Medical doctors, supplies, and bandages were scarce. The battlefield was overflowing with dead soldiers and horses, smashed artillery units, crushed wagons, and burning fires. The confusion of war was compounded by the fact that the average age of a soldier was only fifteen years old.

The Confederate soldiers occupying Gettysburg managed to pull dead horses together to form barricades across the streets. Hiding behind the fortifications of dead horses and sitting in puddles of fresh blood, terrified young soldiers reloaded their muskets and fired aimlessly back at the enemy. Thick clouds of impenetrable smoke rolled through the valley. Confederate sharp shooters perched themselves in tiny attic windows and on balcony ledges, picking off advancing Union soldiers, while Union minie balls showered down upon the town from Cemetery Hill. (The bullet holes are still in the Gettysburg buildings today).

To accommodate the enormous amount of wounded, the warring sides treated the injured anywhere possible. Buildings were turned into makeshift hospitals where both Union and Confederate soldiers were treated on tables next to each other. The dead lay stacked up along the walls, partly to keep them out of the way, and partly to block stray minie balls. In these appalling conditions, even the smallest wound meant death. After the first day of battle came to a confusing close, both sides were shocked by the massive amount of human loss.

As the morning sun slowly ascended on July 2, Union soldiers held the high ground at Big Round Top and Little Round Top along the Cemetery Ridge. Waiting below, Lee's forces began advancing from Seminary Ridge. Their furious assaults were repelled for hours. The Confederate regiments had problems reorganizing and their battle strategies were slow to develop. The Union occupied hills were steeply sloped and the Confederates soldiers were starving, dehydrated, and exhausted.

The soldiers were not just being shot. They were being killed in ways that made them unrecognizable. They spent the entire day tripping over the dead bodies of their friends. Each artillery explosion caused soldiers to fall face first into deep mud. Bellowing soldiers, in close combat, stuck each other with long sharp bayonets. Sword blades swooped through the air slicing throats and opening up bellies.

The massive numbers of those dead grew by the hour. Union cannons brutally cut through the advancing Confederate lines shredding soldiers to pieces. The Union soldiers holding the high ground were also assessing heavy human losses. Occupying the higher ground gave them a good strategic position, but left them with very little cover from the barrage of Confederate artillery. By the end of the second day, the Union positions had withstood the onslaught of enemy advancements. They had held unyielding, but in order to win this battle, each side would have to be willing to pay a grave price.

Death's embrace had taken a tight hold on Gettysburg. Every church, schoolhouse, and home was crammed with hundreds of dying soldiers. The unsanitary conditions were beyond nightmares. Blood, chunks of fleshy tissue, urine, feces, vomit, and decaying corpses swarmed over with millions of flies and mosquitoes. Day old, untreated wounds were already festering with disease. Open-field surgery tents were set up where unclean amputations were done with heavy hacksaws and hot knifes. Infected skin sores turned into festering ulcers the size of dinner plates. The putrid stench of draining puss and bodily excretions was unbearable. The unimaginable scenes of horror intensified as the soldiers moved dismembered body parts out of the way. Soldiers vomited uncontrollably. The heavy clashing sound of war subsided as night's black hand engulfed the battlefield, but there would be no peaceful silence. The wounded screamed and the dying moaned until dawn.

On the morning of July 3rd, the final day of battle, the men awoke to the stench of rotting corpses on the battlefield. Cold and weak, the soldiers reluctantly crawled from their safe campsites and prepared for Hell. The odds were grim, but Robert E Lee was not satisfied with defeat. Lee believed the battle could still be won. The 15,000 remaining Confederate soldiers gathered together for a last ditch effort to strike into the heart of the defending Union forces. In what is now known as Pickets Charge, three divisions of Confederates swiftly stampeded directly at the blue wall of Union forces. The brave Confederate soldiers had to cover almost a mile of wide-open ground while taking direct fire from small arms forces and heavy cannons before they could face the Union troops in a final head-on confrontation. It was an ambitious and devastating assault. While the rushing Confederate soldiers nearly succeed in pushing through the Union brigade, the offensive fell short of success. The Confederate divisions were forced to pull back and Lee had no option left but to call for a full retreat from Gettysburg. The Union forces had won.

For the Confederate army, the horror did not end with the retreat. Their devastated army was hundreds of miles from a solid Confederate stronghold without food or supplies. They were pulling dozens of slow moving wagons stacked with hundreds of wounded soldiers through a very unforgiving wilderness. Sickness and disease ran rampant. Thousands more Confederate soldiers died on the retreating trail. The dead Confederate soldiers left behind on the battlefield were not given the same respect as their Northern counterparts. They were seen as traitors and were purposely left in the open fields to rot away and be eaten by wild animals.

The Confederate army would never recover after the battle of Gettysburg. One third of the mighty Southern Army was lost. The pendulum of fate had swung in the opposite direction. Union forces had never won a major battle before Gettysburg, but following Gettysburg, they would never again lose a major battle. The Union armies pushed back hard and cut through the Confederate controlled states until they eventually won the Civil War.

In the aftermath of Gettysburg, there were over 52,000 casualties and a traumatized community left in utter shambles. The wounded and dying soldiers left behind in tormenting pain had nowhere to go for help and they continued to die in large numbers. Those left alive had the agonizing chore of burying the dead. There was no way that anyone could have been ready for the reality of this situation. Literally thousands of dead soldiers were quickly buried in inadequate mass graves on the battlefield, along the roads, in ditches, and in the lonely fields left unattended and unmarked. Most of the corpses were dug up over the next few years and given a proper burial in military cemeteries in both the North and South. However, it is estimated that there are still more than 1,000 unknown soldiers buried in lost graves throughout Gettysburg. Gettysburg is a town that can never escape its past.

The Soldiers Never Stop Fighting:

Many of the ghosts seen in Gettysburg do not seem to realize that the battle is over. Gettysburg gets millions of tourists from all over the world each year. Most of these tourists visit Gettysburg completely unaware of its history of ghosts. Visitors to the battlefields have reported seeing men dressed in period Civil War uniforms charging forward with their musket and swords drawn and visions of frantic soldiers waving at them to get off the battlefield.

When face to face with a real ghost, most tourists still don't understand what they are seeing. At first, many believe these phantom visions are only reenactment actors playing out a part of the battle. It is not until the ghost vanishes into thin air that the shocked tourists begin to comprehend what they have just witnessed.

The spontaneous manifestation of phantom soldiers on battlefields is not new or even rare. It happens on almost every battlefield throughout the world. The ghosts continue fighting and reenacting their last terrible moments of life trapped in a never-ending cycle. The town of Gettysburg and its buildings, the open fields, the cemeteries, the roads, and the countryside were all part of the battlefield. Don't blink because a ghost can appear anywhere in Gettysburg at any given time.

The Ghost of Jennie Wade:

Jennie Wade, then nineteen years old, was the only known civilian to be killed in the three-day battle. She was in the kitchen of her sister's farmhouse, in the middle of baking bread for the union soldiers, when she was suddenly struck in the back by a stray minie ball that came in through the door, killing her instantly. Jennie's pregnant sister was on a bed only twenty feet away in labor. When another stray minie ball burst through the cabin and struck the bedpost. The bullet fell on the pillow next to her head. Jennie's family carried her lifeless body down into the cellar. Her mother returned upstairs to finish making the bread.

John Wesley Culp, Jennie's close childhood friend, was returning to Gettysburg on July 3rd. He and Jennie had grown very close over the years. Wesley arrived in Gettysburg and visited his sister's house first. He then joined the Union forces in the desperate battle on Culp's Hill. Wesley was mortally wounded in that battle on his family's land. He was dead before Jennie even knew that he had returned, but she would join him only hours later. Jennie died with a picture of John Wesley Culp tucked away in her pocket.

Since that awful day, the cabin where Jennie Wade was killed has been turned into a tourist attraction on Baltimore Street. Guests to the home have experienced strange events such as blue lights coming out of the basement, swinging chains, and moving objects. Odd flickering lights have also been seen in the cabin after closing hours and a white mist that floats through the air and disappears into the rafters. There has even been a story of a tourist who entered the home and went into a trance like state, fell back into a chair, and started talking about past events that only Jennie Wade would have known.

Strange blue lights have also been reported at the nearby gravesite of Jennie Wade located in the Evergreen Cemetery next to the National Cemetery. John Wesley Culp was also laid to rest in Evergreen Cemetery not far away from Jennie.

Paranormal investigators speculate that Jennie Wade is still lingering inside the cabin looking for the life that she never was able to have because of the battle. Many believe that Jennie and Wesley are still searching for each other to say that final goodbye or express lost love. When young people like Jennie Wade and John Wesley Culp are taken away so quickly, the emotional anguish left behind can be extremely powerful- powerful enough to create ghosts.

The Devil's Den:

Devil's Den is a steep rocky hilltop with clusters of enormous granite boulders grouped together surrounded by twisting pathways. The mammoth natural rock formation is both amazing and bewildering. On July 2nd, Confederate sharpshooters overran Union soldiers and strategically positioned themselves within the boulders. The sharpshooters used the position to fire with deadly accuracy on Union soldiers holding nearby Little Roundtop. With an unobstructed view of Plum Run Valley, the fast shooting Confederate snipers caused the valley to be renamed The Valley of Death.

Some of the most powerful photographs of the Civil War were taken at Devil's Den during the Battle of Gettysburg. Some of the best ghost photographs are now being taken at Devil's Den. Investigators entering the area report expensive high tech video equipment failing without explanation. Ghostly voices of terrified soldiers yelling out orders are recorded on tape recorders. Strange lights float over the area. Ghostly wounded apparitions manifest before the eyes of confused tourists. Archeologists, following up on American Indian legends, discovered that the Indians used the granite formation in a large battle of their own long before the Battle of Gettysburg took place. There is also a Shawnee Indian burial mound nearby.

Gettysburg College:

Founded in 1832, the college only consisted of three buildings providing lodging and classrooms for a little more than one hundred students. As the Battle of Gettysburg erupted, the college took on the massive role of providing hospital services for the wounded soldiers. Over six hundred Confederate casualties were treated inside Pennsylvania Hall. Rooms that once educated young minds where now crammed full of dying soldiers. The walls were dripping with blood. Inexperienced doctors conducted surgeries with contaminated instruments and no anesthetic. The solution for most injuries was simple - amputate the limb. Wounded soldiers who were beyond medical treatment were escorted into a lonely room full of dead soldiers to wait for their fate. It was a time of unbearable pain and suffering. The Battle of Gettysburg left the physical and emotional scars behind on the campus buildings.

One of the most famous Gettysburg ghost stories comes from inside Pennsylvania Hall. Two college administrators who worked late one night on the forth floor got into the elevator to leave. Strangely, the elevator passed the designated floor and continued going down to the basement level. The elevator arrived at the basement and the doors opened to a horrifying vision of the past. The basement storage room had been replaced with a brutal hospital scene from 1863.

The sight was silent but horrendous and chaotic. Blood soaked doctors and nurses frantically attended to the enormous amount of wounded soldiers. Dead soldiers were propped up against the walls bleeding from gapping wounds, covering the floors with blood. The panicking administrators immediately pushed frantically at the elevator buttons. As the doors started to close, one of the ghostly orderlies looked directly at the two terrified administrator as if asking them to help. The elevator doors slowly closed and took them back to reality. Both of the administrators were badly shaken by the haunting experience, but continue to work at the campus. However, when they have to work late nights, they both make sure to leave using the steps instead of the elevator.

The campus is full of active apparitions manifesting in front of college staff members and students. Unexplained phantom moans and blood-curdling screams echo the hallways at night. Shadowy figures loom inside buildings only to disappear as people call out or approach them. A Confederate General can be seen walking on the catwalk. There is a civil war soldier who stands guard on top of the cupola. In several instances, this soldier will spot the witness and take aim with his rifle before vanishing. There is even a phantom female siren, a student who committed suicide, whose ghost now beckons to male faculty members and students to come up to the bell tower where she jumped. The story is that this girl's lover was supposed to jump along with her, but changed his mind after watching her jump.

Farnsworth House Inn:

The Farnsworth Inn, built in 1810, is considered by many paranormal investigators to be the most active haunted location in Gettysburg. It's been the feature of many paranormal television programs such as, Sightings, Unsolved Mysteries, and The History Channel.

Confederate soldiers during the Battle of Gettysburg overtook the solid brick inn. The soldiers used a tiny attic window to fire on Union troops atop of Cemetery Hill. Despite the best efforts, the Union sharpshooters could not use their muskets to fire into the tiny window a few hundred yards away. Hundreds of bullet holes are now painted white on the south side of the Farnsworth Inn to highlight the efforts made to shoot the Confederate snipers hidden in the small attic nest.

One of the ghosts still haunting the Farnsworth Inn is a grieving phantom of one of the Confederate snipers. The legend is that this Confederate sniper was perched in the attic window on the final day of the battle. He lined up his musket site on the doorknob of a small cabin down the road and fired a shot trying to determine how much the wind was affecting his shot. The shot went wide missing the target. The minie ball pasted through the wooden doorframe and killed young Jennie Wade. The grief of killing a civilian girl was too much for the Confederate soldier to handle and he committed suicide. The ghostly soldier can be seen wandering through the inn and vanishing through walls.

Another terrible event in the Farnsworth history happened when a little boy was trampled to death by a wagon in front of the inn. The boy was carried inside only to die several days later. The ghost of the little boy can be seen standing alone in rooms or playing in the hallways. There is also a spectral apparition of a weeping man holding a little boy wrapped tightly in a blanket. This is believed to be the ghost of the boy's father still grieving over the loss of his young son.

The most famous ghost haunting the Farnsworth Inn is a vanishing lady known as Mary. Mary had been a housekeeper at the inn. She died in the Sarah Black room, named after a former owner. Unlike most ghosts, Mary seems to intentionally seek out human interaction.

Since her death, visitors have reported seeing Mary dressed in period clothing throughout the house. She wanders the stairways appearing and disappearing before shocked visitors. She has developed the strange habit of sitting on the edge of beds while guests are sleeping. She moves and hides personal items. Mary has even reportedly made appearances during Farnsworth Inn Candlelight Ghost Tours and the Storyteller Theater in the inn's basement. Workers have seen Mary looking into cabinets in the kitchen and waitress's apron strings have been tugged on so hard that the waitresses were spun around.

Other paranormal activity includes the music of a harp that plays in the attic, white balls of light that float through the house, guests hear the singing of a man in the basement as he tries to comfort a dying friend, and abnormal cold spots freeze guests out of rooms. Visitors and workers to the inn have heard the sounds of silverware being placed on empty tables in the middle of the night and seen heavy serving trays raise up into the air under the control of unseen forces before dumping the contents onto the floor.

Today the Farnsworth Inn is open for business. The inn provides lodging, a restaurant, gift shop, Candlelight Ghost Tours, and a Storytellers Theater in the Basement. The list of Gettysburg ghost stories could fill up entire volumes of books. Incredible amounts of pain and misery were dumped onto the landscape creating wounds that time will never mend. Most people cannot comprehend the intense grief and sorrow that blanketed over Gettysburg in 1863.

If you visit Gettysburg, try doing this to help get a better understanding of what it must have been like. Stop anyplace in the town or on the battlefield. Look down at the ground next to your feet. As you're looking at the ground beneath your feet, become aware that someone died a horrible death in the exact spot where you are standing. Then take a couple of steps forward and look down at the ground again. Another poor soul also suffered an agonizing death in that spot.

There is nowhere to avoid the history of death in Gettysburg. Over 52,000 casualties fell in Gettysburg in only three days. There is no place in Gettysburg that is not haunted. It was said once already, but maybe this time it will have more meaning. Gettysburg is a town that can never escape its past.

Mansfield Reformatory- Mansfield, OH

The Guinness Book of World Records lists this massive medieval looking prison, built in 1896, as the world's largest freestanding steel cellblock, having six tiers. Levi T. Scofield, a Cleveland architect, modeled the prison after old world German castles. He built the prison with the intentions of it having a, "spiritual and uplifting architecture," to help better rehabilitate the young men. For much of its existence, the Mansfield Reformatory served as a home to "middle of the road criminals;" young men who were too young for the local boys reformatory and yet not hardened enough to serve time in the maximum security Ohio Penitentiary.

The Reformatory conditions rapidly deteriorated in the mid 1900's until the prison no longer met the modern standards set for federal correctional facilities. The prisoners were slowly transferred to other institutions over the next few decades. The Mansfield Reformatory was finally closed in 1990.

The Mansfield Reformatory Preservation Society (MRPS), who now owns the deed to the prison, was founded and leased the land from the state of Ohio. Since then, Hollywood blockbuster movies like Shawshank Redemption and Air Force One have been filmed on the grounds of the Mansfield Reformatory. MRPS now conducts Hollywood tours and public ghost hunts inside the gothic prison for a set donation to the society.

Since the doors were closed on the Reformatory, there have been legends that the prison is filled with restless spirits of tormented inmates, guards, and prison officials who were never able to leave. As expected with this type of prison, there aregruesome tales of pain, violence, suicides, murders, and other "accidental" deaths. The terrible past events trap the ghosts behind the prisons stonewalls and decaying iron cell bars.

It has been suggested that the architecture of the prison itself draws focus to paranormal energies into the prison. The tops of all of the prison towers are pyramid shaped. They each point toward the large central pyramid tower that spirals down into the heart of the Reformatory. Whatever the reasons behind the prison's ghosts, it becomes clear to visitors that the hallways of the closed Mansfield Reformatory are not as empty as they appear.

The administration wing of the prison was a home and office to Warden Glattke and his wife Helen. Both of them died in this section of the prison. Helen Glattke's death was controversial. Helen accidentally knocked a loaded .32 automatic pistol off a high closet shelf while attempting to remove a jewelry box from the shelf. The gun went off when it hit the floor and the bullet struck Helen killing her instantly.

A decade later, Warden Glattke died of a heart attack in his office. It is believed that both the ghosts of Warden Glattke and his wife Helen haunt the Reformatory. At certain times, visitors can feel cold rushes of air move over their bodies. Strange anomalies are regularly recorded in the administration wing. Photographic orbs and equipment failure are common. The now infamous pink bathroom is also in the administration section. Visitors to the pink bathroom reportedly smell fresh flowers and perfume scents.

The Chapel is another area of the prison were strange events often occur. Video camcorders and other electrical equipment mysteriously fail and shadows seem to move in the darkness. Strange photographs and EVP recordings can be taken in the Chapel. There are rumors that the Chapel room was used as an execution chamber years before it was turned into a Chapel. Inmates were tortured and hung from the rafters. There are reports of a spirit peeking around the doors into the room, pulling away after it is noticed. It is believed that the Chapel, with all of its eerie occurrences, is a main source of the haunting.

There is a hospital infirmary directly above the Chapel. Inmates were treated for and died from horrible diseases like influenza and tuberculosis. Visitors now report feeling strange energies in the air and invisible entities that rush past them and down the stairs. Clusters of orbs can be photographed and EMF detectors can go off the chart. Many of the inmates who died in the infirmary may still haunt the

Reformatory as ghosts.

The basement level is a small maze of dark twisting hallways. The rumor is that prisoners were brought down to the basement to be tortured and beaten. Visitors have reported seeing the ghost of a small boy, 14 years old, presumably beaten to death, standing in the dark hallways. The boy vanishes or runs away seconds after being noticed. There is also the legend of an old ghost named George, a former employee, haunting the basement of the Reformatory.

Not far from the Reformatory is a small graveyard with 215 numbered markers. These are inmates that went unclaimed after death. They are buried here alone with a number instead of a name. The graveyard is off limits to visitors because it is still owned by the new, adjacent correctional facility. The cemetery can be seen from the top of the guard tower, where witnesses have seen objects mysteriously fall or move without explanation.

A female ghost haunts the Reformatory's library. This ghost is allegedly either Helen Glattke, the Warden's wife, or the ghost of a young nurse who was supposedly killed by an inmate. Many psychics experience the vision of a young woman inside the prison. Visitors to the library have felt sick and light headed. Equipment stops working without warning and bizarre photographs often show strange lights and dramatic orbs.

The library is just another room in the enormous fortress of the Mansfield Reformatory. The east and west cellblocks are vast caves of decaying iron bars, chipping paint, and filthy mattresses. The cell doors are all open, but the ghosts remain imprisoned.

Murders and suicides occurred in the cellblocks. Inmates tied bed sheets around their necks and then twisted them around the bars until they strangled themselves to death. Other inmates were thrown off of the higher tiers for something as trivial as a pack of cigarettes. Life inside a prison is hard and filled with hate, wickedness, and agony. The ghosts haunting these cellblocks are still dealing with the same emotions and hardships that they struggled with everyday of their life. The building has changed, but the negative feelings continue.

The prison's most violent events happened in 1957 after a prison riot. An estimated 120 inmates were sentenced to thirty days in The Hole. The Hole was solitary confinement in a basement level of the prison equipped with only twenty cell units. The legend is that two men went into a cell and only one came out alive. The bodies of the murdered inmates were tucked away under the beds. The Hole is a place that has witnessed the darkest side of human nature. The negative energies left behind make this area one of the most significant haunted hearts inside the prison.

A visitor to The Hole does not have to be psychic to experience the intense residual forces. Many visitors who venture into The Hole become sick to their stomach, the hairs stand up on the back of their necks, goose bumps run up and down their arms, ghostly footsteps follow them, and they can't help feeling like they are being watched.

Maybe visitors are being watched. Many have reported seeing glowing eyes peering back at them from the darkness. Orbs can be photographed or videotaped. Many people have recorded strange sounds and scary voices on EVP recorders. The "impressions" left in the atmosphere and the ghostly activity experienced in The Hole are the genuine results of years of traumatic fear and terror.

Exploring the entire Mansfield Reformatory can be physically and mentally exhausting. Witnessed events are hard to account for with reasonably logical explanations. Paranormal investigators continue traveling to this old prison searching for its hidden secrets. Mansfield Reformatory's darkest secret might be the fact that even in death, some souls do not find freedom.

West Virginia State Penitentiary

After West Virginia seceded from Virginia in 1863, the new state made plans to construct their own maximum-security prison. State legislation purchased a twenty-acre plot of land on the edge of Moundsville for their new penitentiary. When construction was finished in 1876, the prison resembled a gothic fortress. The twenty-four foot high, six-foot wide walls were produced with hand cut sandstone taken from a local quarry. The unique architecture is adorned with huge turrets and medieval battlements. The ominous looking penitentiary looms over the town of Moundsville.

Old prison systems all have horrific stories of unspeakable events like botched riots, violent murders, and human atrocities. The West Virginia State Penitentiary is no different. The penitentiary was used to imprison some of the worst criminals in the state. The inmates were kept confined to tiny 5 x 7 cells for twenty-two hours a day. They were only let out of their cells for light exercise in a specially designed restricted yard that was completely surrounded by a strong chain link fence, razor wire, and snipers. Even daily meals were eaten in the cells.

In the early days of the prison, the focus was on prisoner rehabilitation. Inmates were educated and given the opportunity to learn trade skills. However, by the 1960's, the inmate population had exploded and the amount of violent criminals became too difficult to manage. State funding was at an all time low causing the penitentiary to begin a steady process of physical deterioration.

The most violent day in the prisons history occurred on New Years Day in 1986 when the inmate's launched a full-scale prison riot. The riot was a success and the inmates took sixteen correctional officers hostage. A special negotiating team ended the violent confrontation with no harm coming to any of the hostages, but three inmates were murdered.

The prisoners rioted in protest of the decaying conditions inside the penitentiary. Lawyers for the prisoners had already filed six different lawsuits against the penitentiary, but years passed as the case slowly filtered through endless red tape. Finally, after the riot, The West Virginia Supreme Court agreed with the prisoners. They ruled that the penitentiary violated the prisoners' Eighth Amendment rights, which prohibit cruel and unusual punishment, and violated the inmates' right to be rehabilitated. The penitentiary closed its gates in 1995 and all of the remaining prisoners were moved to the newly built Mt. Olive Correctional Center.

Some of the most famous haunted rooms in the penitentiary include Snake Eyes, The Death Row House, and the Sugar Shack.

The Snake Eyes room got its name from a painting of a pair of dice on one of its walls created by an inmate. The room was used during the 1986 prison riot to store the dead bodies of the inmates executed in the Sugar Shack. Snake Eyes also had a twisting staircase leading up to the South Hallway. The stairs gave the prisoners a blind spot away from the view of the guards. Many inmates were murdered on the stairs until prison officials finally closed off the staircase from further use.

Before the stairs were sealed off, one unlucky inmate was found with this throat slit ear to ear. Snake Eyes is filled with terrifying screams that echo the empty hallways and dark ghostly shadows that cry out in pain. The anger and hate have formed some powerful locations in the Penitentiary where desperate ghosts now roam in the darkness. Unexplainable cold spots pass through the room.

The Death Row House did not have many cells. The penitentiary was very good at conducting state sanctioned executions keeping the death row population low. There was a "nothing to lose" attitude in death row, which led to over two-dozen murders committed by inmates who were settling old scores. There was little punishment for inmate murders in death row. After all, what could the state do to punish these hardened criminals? Kill them twice?

From 1899 to 1959, the penitentiary executed ninety-five men. Eighty-five death row inmates were put to death by hanging and nine were electrocuted. Capital punishment in West Virginia banned in 1965. The death house was torn down, but the electric chair, arrogantly named Old Sparky, is currently on exhibit inside the penitentiary.

The most famous room in the penitentiary is the Sugar Shack. The prison guards feared this room and almost never entered it. The room was a basement area crammed with hundreds of violent inmates. The inmates played cards, dice, and billiards. They also often fought, raped, and murdered each other. The Sugar Shack is also the room where rioting inmates set up a mock trial and sentenced three of their fellow inmates to brutal deaths. One of the unfortunate condemned men had his heart slowly cut out. The three dead inmates were dumped into the Snake Eyes room.

The Sugar Shack is the one room in the penitentiary where many paranormal events recorded border on demonic or evil. The negative energy flowing through this

area of the prison is very intense. The putrid stench of sulfur can fill the room making visitors gag and vomit. Voices whisper around the living as if they are plotting evil actions against them. Sinister laughing and angry, unknown voices cursing aloud cause most guests to run away from the Sugar Shack and the penitentiary.

The penitentiary was a melting pot for negative energy. The ghosts of the prisoners left behind continue to carry with them all of the rage and hatred of their own wicked lives. Many unsuspecting visitors to the penitentiary experience overwhelming feelings of dread and panic causing them to leave the prison. The West Virginia State Penitentiary's dark past makes it a mysterious site and one of the most haunted prisons in the world.

Paranormal Organizations

Academy of Religion and Psychical Research
P.O. Box 614, Bloomfield, CT 06002-0614
Tel: (860) 242-4593
http://www.lightlink.com/arpr/

American Ghost Society
515 East Third Street, Alton, Illinois - 62002
Tel: (618) 465-1086
http://www.prairieghosts.com/

American Society for Psychical Research (ASPR)
5 West 73rd Street, New York, New York 10023
Tel: (212) 799-5050
http://www.aspr.com/

Australian Ghost Hunters Society
Eoghan Arnold (Melbourne), President
Rowena Gilbert (Sydney), Vice President
PO Box 49 Seddon West, Victoria, 3011 Australia
http://www.aghs.org.au/

Berkeley Psychic Institute
2018 Allston Way, Berkeley, CA 94704
Tel: (510) 548-8020
http://www.berkeleypsychic.com/

(British) Society for Psychical Research
49 Marloes Road, Kensington, London W8 6LA
Tel: 020 7937 8984
http://www.spr.ac.uk/

The College of Psychic Studies (UK)
16 Queensberry Place, London SW7 2EB
Tel: +44 (0)20 7589 3292
http://www.psychic-studies.org.uk/

(CSICOP) Committee for the Scientific Investigation of Claims of the Paranormal
Box 703, Amherst, NY, 14226
Tel: 716-636-1425
http://www.csicop.org/

The Ghost Club (UK)
PO Box 24268, London SE9 6XL
Chairman, Alan Murdie
chairman@ghostclub.org.uk
http://www.ghostclub.org.uk/

(GRS) Ghost Research Society
Dale Kaczmarek, President.
PO Box 205 Oak Lawn, IL 60454-0205
Tel: (708) 425-5163
http://www.ghostresearch.org/

International Ghost Hunters Society
Dr. Dave Oester & Rev. Sharon Gill, Co-Founders.
IGHS Ghost Headquarters
Crooked River Ranch, OR 97760
Tel: 541-548-4418
http://www.ghostweb.com/

(ISPR) International Society for Paranormal Research
Parapsychologist Dr. Larry Montz, Founder, 1972.
4712 Admiralty Way # 541 Marina del Rey, CA 90292
Tel: (323) 644-8866
http://www.hauntings.com/

Koestler Parapsychology Unit
Department of Psychology
University of Edinburgh
7, George Square, Edinburgh EH8 9JZ, United Kingdom
Tel: +44 (0)131 650 3348
http://moebius.psy.ed.ac.uk/

New England Society for Psychic Research
Ed and Lorraine Warren, Directors.
P.O. Box 41, Monroe, CT 06468
http://www.warrens.net/

Parapsychology Foundation, Inc.
228 East 71st Street, New York NY 10021 USA
Tel: 212-628-1550
http://www.parapsychology.org/

Princeton Engineering Anomalies Research
C-131, Engineering Quadrangle
Princeton University, Princeton, NJ 08544
Tel: (609) 258-5950
http://www.princeton.edu/~pear/

Rhine Research Center
402 N. Buchanan Blvd., Durham, NC 27701-1728
Tel: (919) 688-8241
http://www.rhine.org/

The Skeptics Society and Skeptics Magazine
P.O. Box 338, Altadena, CA 91001
Tel: (626) 794-3119
http://www.skeptic.com/

Zerotime Paranormal Research
Trent Brandon, Founder
Based in Ohio, USA
http://www.zerotime.com/

Quick Reference Guide

Agent: A human being, typically a teenage female, who unknowingly directs poltergeist energy.

Altered State of Consciousness (ASC): Any state of consciousness that is different from "normal" states of waking or sleeping.

Amulet: An object that has the power to ward off ghosts and evil spirits.

Angel: Benevolent spiritual beings who help and watch over people.

Apparition: The disembodied soul or spirit that can be seen visually.

Apport: When a solid object seemingly appears from out of nowhere, with the help of the spirits in the presence of a medium.

Asport: When a solid object is teleported to a different location with the help of the spirits in the presence of a medium.

Astral Body: The soul of an individual projected outside of their bodies.

Astral Projection: See Out-Of-Body (OBE).

Atmospheric Apparition: Not actually a ghost or spirit, but instead a "visual imprint" of people and events that was left behind in the environment that continues to replay.

Aura: A field of energy believed by some to surround living creatures.

Automatic Writing: A type of communication with ghosts or spirits where they take control over the writer's hand and write out a message.

Automatism: An unconscious or spontaneous muscular movement caused by ghosts or the spirits. Automatic Writing is one form of Automatism.

Banshee: Omen spirits of Scotland and Ireland.

Channeling: A form of spirit communication where an unseen entity possesses a medium in a controlled environment to impart guidance, wisdom or future events. The channeled entity could be a deceased human being, an Angel, Demon, Elemental or other higher plain spirit.

Charms: A spell or object possessing magic power.

Clairvoyance: Either an internal or external vision of present or future events, objects, places, and people.

Cold Reading: A psychic reading given with no prior knowledge of the sitter.

Collective Apparition: A ghost or spirit sighting simultaneously by more than one living person.

Collective Unconscious: Form of analytical psychology developed by Carl Jung. It is the collective memory of all the humanity's past and is held somewhere inside the unconscious mind.

Crisis Apparition: Ghosts that appear to loved ones and close friends just before or soon after their death.

Cross Correspondence: Information received from the spirit world.

Crossroads: Point where two roads intersect. Said to be a focus point of supernatural energy.

Death Bed Apparitions: See Crisis Apparition.

Demon: Fallen angels associated with evil.

Direct Voice Phenomenon (DVP): The voice of a ghost or spirit being spoken to the sitters of a séance. The voice usually comes from some point near the medium, but not through the medium. Sometimes a spirit horn or trumpet is used.

Direct Writing: When ghost or spirit's handwriting appears directly on a previously unmarked, unwritten surface.

Drop-In Communicator: A ghost, spirit or entity that makes its presence known at a séance.

Dowsing: The paranormal detection of underground water or mineral deposits (or lost persons and objects) using a divining rod or pendulum.

Dybbuk: A Jewish legend. The restless soul of a deceased human being that enters the body of a living person and takes possession.

Earth Lights: Luminous phenomena typically shaped in ball form or irregular patches of light appearing randomly and defying explanation.

Ectoplasm: Ectoplasm can be either a solid, liquid or vaporous substance produced by ghosts or spirits. It is usually a milky white color and has an ozone smell. Some forms of ectoplasm are known to move in lifelike patterns.

Electronic Voice Phenomena (EVP): EVP is the attempt to capture a ghost or spirits voice on audio recording tapes. Typically there is no voice heard to the people present at the recording but after reviewing the tapes there are strange voices recorded.

Electro-Magnetic Field (EMF) Detectors: Handheld scientific instruments that can pick up electronic and magnetic fields over different frequencies. They can read changes and distortions in the normal electro-magnetic fields.

Elemental Spirit: A spirit associated with one of the classical four elements (fire, earth, air and water).

Extrasensory Perception (ESP): The acquisition of information by means beyond the five human senses.

Exorcism: A religious rite used to cast out a ghost, spirit or entity from a living persons body or a particular location.

Exorcist: A religious "holy man" who conducts an exorcism.

Fairy: Small, human-like mythical being. May be benevolent or malevolent.

False Awakening: An experience in which a person believes he or she has woken up, but actually is still dreaming.

Family Apparitions: Ghosts that haunt one particular family. Their appearance usually means that someone within the family is about to die.

Focal Person: Person who is at the center of poltergeist activity.

Ghost: The visual appearance of a spirit or soul of a deceased being, human or animal. The disembodied soul or lifeforce.

Ghost Catcher: A wind chime like device that makes noise as a ghost or spirit passes by it.

Ghost Hunt: An attempt made by the living to find and see a ghost or spirit.

Ghost Hunter: A living individual who searches out and sometime finds and identifies ghosts and spirits.

Ghost Investigation: A scientific endeavor, in a controlled environment, set up to communicate, record, and capture visual evidence of the existence of ghosts.

Ghost Lights: See Earth Lights.

Ghostbuster: A living person who can remove an unwanted ghost, spirit, entity or poltergeist activity from a particular location.

Ghoul: Evil spirit or monster that robs graves and feeds off of the flesh of the dead.

Gray Lady: The ghost of a woman who has died at the hands of a lover or waits for the return of a loved one.

Guardian Angel: An angel believed to protect the individual.

Halloween: All Hallows Eve, is the night of October 31st when the spirit and normal world allegedly become one.

Hallucination: A false and distorted perception of reality.

Haunt: A place where a ghost or ghosts frequently return.

Haunting: The continuous manifestation of inexplicable phenomena associated with the presence of ghosts or spirits attached to a particular location.

Haunted Objects: Jewelry, furniture, clothing, etc, that seem to be haunted by a past owner or have been cursed.

Hitchhikers: Spirits and other supernatural entities that attach themselves to people, objects or other supernatural entities for the purpose of moving from one place to another. Hitchhikers can stowaway between dimensions, or between locations in the same dimension.

Hypnotism: An induced trance or sleep state.

Ley Lines: Invisible lines that run between sacred objects or locations.

Levitation: The paranormal raising or suspension of an object or person.

Lucid Dreams: A dream where the dreamer does not know that they are dreaming.

Luminous Phenomena: The experience of strange lights or glows, often around objects or people.

Magnetometer: A technical device used to study the strength, direction and fluctuation of magnetic fields.

Marian Apparition: The appearance of the Virgin Mary.

Materialization: The manifestation of physical objects, animals or people.

Medium: A person with a gift to communicate with ghosts and spirits on behalf of the living.

Modern Apparitions: "New" Ghosts of deceased individuals. They appear in fashion from the current time.

Near-Death Experience (NDE): A phenomenon in which a person clinically dies or comes very close to death only to be revived and then can recall in great detail stories of spiritual worlds and other supernatural events.

Necromancer: A person usually considered a wizard or sorcerer, who can raise the dead and command the spirits to obtain information about the future.

Necromancy: A form of prophecy preformed by a necromancer.

Omen: A foretelling of a future event.

Oracle: A seer who can communicate with ghosts, spirits and Gods to obtain information.

Ouija Board: A board with letters and numbers used by people who are attempting to communicate with ghosts or spirits.

Out-Of-Body (OBE): Also called Astral Projection. The phenomenon in which a living person's spirit can exit their body, travel the earth and other spiritual worlds and then return back to their bodies.

Paranormal: Beyond the normal.

Parapsychology: The scientific study of unusual events associated with the human experience and PSI subjects.

Percipient: A living person who sees a ghost, spirit or paranormal event.

Phantom Animals: Ghosts of deceased animals.

Phantom Hitchhiker or Traveler: A ghost or spirit that haunts a particular stretch of road or route. Phantom Hitchhikers ask for rides only to suddenly disappear when they reach their destination.

Photographic Apparitions: Ghosts and spirits that you can't see, but appear in photographs after they are developed.

Planchette: A pointer used with a Ouija Board to communicate with ghosts, spirits or higher plane entities.

Poltergeist: "Noisy Ghost." Poltergeists are invisible masses of spirit energy that may or may not be connected to a living human Agent. Some of the most common poltergeists activities include loud unexplained noise, levitations, the moving of objects, and electrical problems.

Possession: When a persons mind and body are taken over by ghosts, spirits or other supernatural entities such as demons.

Precognition: The paranormal awareness of future events.

PSI: A general term used to denote the unknown factors responsible for a variety of paranormal phenomena.

Psychic: Popular term used to denote a person who regularly uses, or who appears to be especially gifted with psi abilities.

Psychic Echo: When sounds from the past have mysteriously recorded themselves into the natural environment.

Psychokinesis (PK): Mind Movement. Psychokinesis (PK) is the apparent ability to influence the environment by intention alone.

Purgatory: The place where the souls of those who have died must go to be cleansed of all their sin before they can be admitted to Heaven.

Radio Voice Phenomenon (RVP): The voice of a ghost or spirit communicating through a regular radio.

Reciprocal Apparition: An experience where both the agent and the ghost or spirit see and react to each other.

Recurring Apparitions: Ghosts or spirits that appear in regular cycles, usually once a year, on the anniversary of their death, for example.

Reincarnation: The belief that a soul can be reborn into a new body after death.

Repressed Psychokinetic Energy: A theoretical psychic force unconsciously produced by an individual while undergoing a physical or mental trauma.

Retrocognition: Paranormal knowledge of past events.

Scrying: A type of prophecy where an individual can see future events by staring into a shiny or reflective surface, such as a mirror or crystal ball.

Séance: The gathering of a group of individuals for the purpose of communicating with the dead.

Sensitive: Someone who is aware or can detect paranormal events beyond the range of their five human senses.

Screaming Skulls: Human skulls that protest with poltergeist activity when their final wishes are not fulfilled.

Shaman: A witchdoctor or medicine man who communicates with spirits while in trance and who has the power of healing.

Sixth sense: Popular term for ESP.

Sleep Paralysis: A frightening state of seeming to being awake but unable to move.

Soul: The spiritual lifeforce or essence, carrying an individual's personality and consciousness of all actions.

Spectre: A ghost or apparition.

Spirit: Often used to define the soul of a person, but it can also be used to represent places such as sacred lakes or objects, shrines, and elemental entities.

Spirit Detection: The reading made by scientific equipment (EMF Detectors, Temperature changes, etc.) when a ghost or spirit is present.

Spirit Photography: Photographs of figures or faces, believed by some to be those of deceased persons.

Spirit Profile: Researching the background and history of the ghost or spirit, then determining its consistent patterns as a result of the findings.

Spiritualism: Belief systems that ghosts and spirits can and do communicate with the living.

Spook Lights: See Earth Lights.

Stigmata: Unexplained markings on a person's body that correspond to the wounds of Christ.

Super-ESP: A more powerful form of telepathy that allow certain individuals to pick up information about a deceased person from other living people.

Supernatural: Something that exists or occurs through some means other than any known force in nature or science.

Time-Slips: Moments where the past and present collide at one point.

Telepathy: Mind-to-mind communication.

Telephone Calls From The Dead: When a person receives a telephone call from someone who is dead. The person may or may not know that the caller is deceased.

Teleportation: Paranormal transportation of an object from one location to another, even through solid objects.

Transportation Apparitions: The appearance of ghostly cars, trucks, ships, bicycles, carriages, trains, airplanes and anything else that carry people. They haunt their old routes.

Vampire: A supernatural creature (undead) that can only come out at night and lives by drinking the blood of the living.
Wild Hunt: A group of ghost horsemen or packs of ghostly dogs seen at night.

Witch: A women with supernatural powers.

Wraith: A ghost that comes back to avenge its own death. Considered an omen spirit.

References

Alcock, E. James. *Parapsychology: Science or Magic? A Psychological Perspective.* Oxford: Pergamon, 1981.

Anson, Jay. *The Amityville Horror.* Prentice Hall 1977.

Arcangel, Dianne & Moody, Raymond A. Jr. *Life After Loss : Conquering Grief and Finding Hope.* San Francisco: Harper, 2001.

Ashley, R.N. Leonard. *The Complete Book of Devils and Demons.* New York: Barricade Books, 1996.

Auerbach, Loyd. *ESP, Hauntings and Poltergeists: A Parapsychologist's Handbook.* New York: Warner Books, 1986.

Banks, Ivan. *Enigma of Borley Rectory: Britain's Most Haunted House.* January 1996

Bayless, Raymond. *The Enigma of the Poltergeist.* West Nyack, NY: Parker Publishing Co., 1967.

Bells, Charles Bailey. *The Bell Witch.* Nashville, 1934.

Clough, A.H. (editor), Dryden, John (translator). *Plutarch : Lives of Noble Grecians and Romans, Vol. 1 (Modern Library Series).* Modern Library, 1992.

The Holy Bible. New York: The World Publishing Company.

Braude, E. Stephen. *The Limits of Influence: Psychokinesis and the Philosophy of Science.* University Press of America. Revised Edition 1997.

Brough, R. *Parapsychology: The Controversial Science.* New York: Ballantine Books 1991.

Clark, Jerome. *Unexplained!* Canton, MI: Visible Ink Press, 1999.

Cohen, Daniel. *The Encyclopedia of Ghosts.* New York: Dodd, Mead & Co., 1984.

Dingwall, E.J., Kathleen M. Goldney and Trevor H. Hall. *Haunting of Borley Rectory.* London: Gerald Duckworth, 1956.

Fox H. Richard, and Cunningham L. Carl. *Crime Scene Search and Physical Evidence Handbook.* Boulder, Colorado: Paladin Press, 1992

Friedman Russell & James, John W. *The Grief Recovery Handbook : The Action Program for Moving Beyond Death, Divorce, and Other Losses.* HarperCollins, Revised Edition (June 1998).

Gross, Michael. *The Evidence for Phantom Hitchhikers.* Wellingborough, Northamptonshire, England: The Aquarian Press, 1984.

Guiley, Rosemary Ellen. *Harper's Encyclopedia of Mystical & Paranormal Experience.* Edison, New Jersey: Castle Books, 1991.
Guiley, Rosemary Ellen. *The Encyclopedia of Ghosts and Spirits.* New York: Facts on File, 1992.

Guiley, Rosemary Ellen. *The Encyclopedia of Witches and Witchcraft.* New York: Facts on File, 1989.

Haining, Peter. *A Dictionary of Ghosts.* London, 1982.

Harkleroad, Tim. *The Complete Haunted House Book.* Bristol, TN: Moonlighting Publications, 1998.

Harry, Price. *The Most Haunted House in England.* New York: Time-Life Books (reprint), 1990.

Hauch, Dennis William. *Haunted Places: The National Directory.* New York: Penguin Books, 1996.

Hunt, Stoker. *Ouija : The Most Dangerous Game.* Barnes & Noble, 1992.

Jordan, Michael. *Witches - An Encyclopedia of Paganism and Magic.* North Pomfret, Vermont: Trafalgar Square, 1998.

Kaplan, Stephen, PhD and Kaplan, Salch Roxanne. *The Amityville Horror Conspiracy.* Toad Hall Inc. 2nd Ed edition 1995.

Kovach Sue. *Hidden Files: Law Enforcement's True Case Stories of the Unexplained and Paranormal.* Chicago, Illinios: Contemporary Book Publishing, 1998.

MacKenzie, Andrew. *Hauntings and Apparitions.* London: Heinemann Ltd., 1982.

MacKenzie, Andrew. *The seen and the Unseen.* London: Weidenfeld & Nicolson, 1987.

Nesbitt, Mark. *Ghosts of Gettysburg I, II, III, IV, V.* Thomas Publications. Gettysbury, PA, 1991-2000

Sellier E. Charles, and Meier, Joe. *The Paranormal Sourcebook : A Complete Guide to All Things Otherworldly.* Lowell House, 1999

Taylor, Troy. *The Ghost Hunter's Handbook.* Alton, Illinios: WhiteChapel Productions, Second Edition 1998.

Time Life Books. *Mysteries of the Unknown: Phantom Encounters.* Alexandria, Virginia: Time Life Books, 1988.

Underwood, Peter. *Gazetteer of British, Scottish, and Irish Ghosts.* New York: Bell Publishing Co., 1985

Underwood, Peter. *Ghosts and How to See Them.* Osnaburgh Street, London: Anaya Publishers Limited, 1993.

Underwood, Peter. *The Ghost Hunter's Guide.* Park Avenue, New York: Sterling Publishing Company, 1987.

Warren, Ed. Warren Lorraine. *The Demonologist.*

Wilber, Ken. *Quantum Questions: Mystical Writings of the World's Great Physicists.* Boulder, Colorado: Shambhala, 1984.
Wilson, Colin. *Afterlife.* London, 1985.

Wilson, Colin. *Poltergeist; A Study in Destructive Haunting.* St. Paul, Minnesota: Llewellyn Publications, 1993.

Music Copyright and Trademark References:

Urge Overkill. Stull [EP] [EP]. Touch & Go (Exclusive), Audio CD Original Release Date: June 30, 1992

Product Trademark References:

Ouija, and *Ouija Board* are registered Trademarks of Parker Brothers.

Movie Copyright and Trademark References:

Poltergeist. Co-producer/co-writer Steven Spielberg, Director Tobe Hopper: MGM Studios Inc. 1982.

The Exorcist. Written by William Peter Blatty, Director William Friedkin: Warner Bros. 1973.

Addendum
More Ghost Hunting Information

Using Psychics on Ghost Hunts

Psychic abilities can be helpful tools. However, just like any other tool, there is a right way and a wrong way to use them. Used correctly, psychic abilities can be a ghost-hunting asset. If ghost hunters do not understand the nature of psychic abilities and use psychics incorrectly, the process tends to be a waste of important time. The information gathered from a true psychic can be extremely valuable or utterly worthless depending solely on how the ability is utilized.

There are many dos and don'ts when using a psychic. Psychics should always be used in a separate control group on any ghost hunt. A separate person should stay with them to take notes and record what the psychic experiences. Psychics should enter a ghost hunt with only their own abilities. No one should provide the psychic with any information. Unlike regular ghost hunters, it is important for a psychic to know as little information as possible about a location before going on a ghost hunt. Ghost hunters should know everything possible about a location. For psychics, too much information can contaminate thoughts or lead them to false judgments. No one should answer specific questions that the psychic may have about a location. The psychic should not use magical rituals before or during the ghost hunts or ask other people to control energy or concentrate.

It is not a good idea to have psychics close to scientific equipment like EMF detectors because such devices tend to make audio sounds while picking up data. The visual and audio effects of the equipment and the people using the equipment can be misleading to a psychic. In the back of the psychic's mind, they may think the alarm went off on the ghost hunting equipment because something supernatural is happening. Obviously, that is not always the case, but it can be a guiding factor in the mind of a psychic. Jumping to a rash conclusion too quickly happens all of the time, even to veteran ghost hunters. Psychics are not immune to having the same type of outside interference distort their rational reasoning.

Psychics do have limitations that ghost hunters and the psychics themselves should know about and keep in mind. Psychics rarely ever crack the fifty percent ratio. This means that in any controlled test using the psychic's own ability (telepathy, clairvoyance, precognition, psychometric, etc.) the psychic is incorrect more than half of the time. However, true psychics do tend to have a higher percentage than someone who is guessing, which is an important fact to note because it shows that there is increased accuracy beyond the average percentage.

Many psychic abilities tend not to work in confusing environments. They appear to be inherently connected to the emotions of the psychic. Scientific experiments done at the world's leading parapsychology organizations have shown that heightened human emotions decrease the accuracy of psychic abilities. Nervousness, excitement, depression, anxiety, and fear all have negative results on psychic abilities. Heightened emotional states happen to everyone, psychic and non-psychic, on a ghost hunt. For a psychic, the key to success is to remain in full control of their emotions on a ghost hunt, which in many cases could be an impossible task.

There is also a chance of misidentifying the emotions a psychic feels at a location. A psychic can be at a murder scene and experience feelings of anger, hatred, rage, and violence. Often, there is then a misinterpretation that the ghost haunting this location is the one filled with these dark feelings of rage. However, the ghost can be one of the innocent murdered victims and is in no way malicious toward the living. The problem is that the psychic is picking up the residual energy imprints that were left behind from the murder itself and not the emotions of the ghost. When a psychic says that they feel anger or hatred, it does not necessarily mean that the ghosts feel this way. The psychic could be reading the leftover energy from a past event

Another limitation with psychics is that many of them do not understand their own psychic abilities. Psychics usually do not see an exact mental image of a person, place, or event. Their visions tend to occur in an abstract manner. They will see colors and shapes or feel emotions. Then their mind will interpret these random psychic flashes to mean something other than what they actually are based on the psychic's personal assumptions. The interpretation is where the problem lies. Personal interpretation leaves an enormous amount of room for error.

Here is an example of a real psychic test that shows that normal human presumptions can play a large role in a psychic's final interpretation:

A psychic is asked to sit in a room while another person, the subject in this experiment, travels around outside of the room. The psychic is not given any information about where the subject is going. They are asked to use their psychic ability to determine where the subject is traveling and what is happening around them.

The subject decides to go downtown to a local dog show. The psychic feels that the subject is walking on a hard surface like a sidewalk, which the subject is at the time. The psychic then sees a vision of bright colors and giant words on a large banner at the same time that the subject is approaching the dog show. The building has large colorful banners draped across the front. The psychic senses the presence of animals simultaneously as the subject is walking next to the dogs. When the subject orders some food, the psychic says that they can taste food. Then the subject leaves the dog show and buys some roses from a street vendor to give to his wife. The psychic says that they can smell fresh flowers. At this point, it would seem that the psychic was incredibley accurate. However, the experiment is not over yet.

The psychic is given a folder with twenty-five photographs. The photographs are random places throughout the city. The psychic is told that one of the photographs is the location where the subject has been. The psychic is asked to pick out the correct photograph from the group. A photograph of the building where the dog show took place is in the group. The photograph is of the plain looking building without the fancy advertising banners and dogs. After reflection, the psychic chooses a photograph taken at the local zoo.

The psychic did not select the correct photograph because they were not using their psychic ability. Instead, they relied on their interpretations of the psychic images. The psychic felt the subject walk on concrete, look at a colorful banner, enter the presence of animals, eat food, and smell flowers. The psychic then determined, as anyone else would, that all of those experiences could be found at the zoo. The psychic did not consider any of the other photographs because they did not seem to meet the criteria of their psychic visions. Remember, the psychic did not see an absolute picture, but abstract glimpses and small pieces of a larger puzzle. The final photograph choice had nothing to do with psychic abilities and everything to do with the natural preconceptions of the psychic. Psychics can see different visions at a single location then misinterpret those images and end up with an absolutely wrong conclusion.

There are things that ghost hunters should not expect from a psychic. Ghost hunters should not expect psychics to enter a location and automatically have visions come to them. That is not how psychic abilities work, except in Hollywood movies. No one should rush the psychic through the process. The psychic should be given whatever time needed to complete the connection. No one should try to force the psychic to have experiences. If the psychic experiences something that is too disturbing for them to handle, someone should escort the psychic from the location before continuing the investigation. The safety and feelings of the living should always come first during any ghost hunt.

After a ghost hunt, the psychic should give the team leader a complete account of everything they felt, saw, heard, and experienced on the investigation and exactly where everything was experienced. The team leader should then evaluate the information provided by the psychic and try to match it up to other known facts about the location or ghost. Ghost hunters should be looking for a correlation or a link between the psychic data and the known facts. If the facts of a case are that a seventeen-year-old girl's jealous boyfriend murdered her inside her bedroom thirty-five years ago and her ghost has been reportedly seen by passersby standing in the front yard in a white nightgown crying; that case has a lot of good factual information that can be verified by a psychic, but the psychic should not know about any of that information before or during their visit to the location. The psychic must rely on his or her own uncontaminated psychic abilities to uncover knowledge about the case, which can be later verified through historical information or an eyewitness testimony.

After the team leader has had time to evaluate the information provided by the psychic, they should interview (not interrogate) the psychic. The interviews should be recorded on audio or video for future reference. If a psychic reports details that cannot be verified at the time, that does not necessarily mean that they are incorrect. These details may prove to be accurate and valuable at a future date when more information becomes available. It is extremely important for ghost hunters to understand the psychic process. By understanding psychic abilities and the psychics that use them, a ghost hunter will develop their own intuition about when and how to use psychics to aid the ghost hunting process.

Seeing Ghostly Faces in Photographs

Many ghost hunter's rush to judgment when presented with an image that seems to resemble a human face. Recognizing faces in ambiguous patterns such as photographs, wood textures, clouds, and even in food is common and completely normal. These faces are often nothing more than obscure textures and shadow tricks that happen to line up in just the right way so that the human brain registers the images as a face. This is a natural process with a psychological explanation. The illusion is called pareidolia, which is the misperception of an obscure stimulus being perceived as something more specific and distinct. Basically, it is an innate human characteristic to see something in something else. Examples would include seeing the image of an angel on a burrito or seeing the face of the devil in a puff of smoke. The human mind has developed a system to identify faces as a survival method. Facial detection helps keep humans from being surprised and attacked by predators.

Faces can be seen in many everyday objects. The wood grain on doors can create evil looking faces. Faces can be identified on the bark texture of an old tree. The headlight placement on the front of a car might make the car appear angry. The telltale windows (eyes) of the famous Amityville house give it the distinctly dreadful appearance of a menacing face. Ghost hunters should keep this information in mind and grow to be skeptical about the faces seen in photographs. Human vision is very susceptible to optical illusions. What a ghost hunter believes they are seeing might not be what they are actually seeing.

Not every person's visual connection works in exactly the same way. Some people can see faces in just about any image while other people will look at the same photograph and never see anything unless it is suggested. Stereograms are a good example of an optical illusion. A stereogram is a 3D image hidden within what seems like a mass of random shapes and colors. When viewed in the correct way, the stereogram produces the impression of a concealed image. Some people will look at a stereogram and see the hidden image right away while others can stare at the picture all day and their brains will not process the information in a manner to allow them to visualize the image.

Ghost hunters want to see something in photographs. That is why they take pictures in the first place. When there is something in the photograph that seems to have a distinguishing pair of eyes, a nose, and a mouth, the natural conclusion is to believe that a ghost has been captured on film. Closer examination usually shows that the light, shadows, reflections, shades of colors, and random textures are combining in a way to create a false image. Now this does not mean that if there is an unexplainable looking face in a photograph that the face is absolutely not something supernatural, but that the image should be rationally examined and analyzed for the best reasonable conclusion.

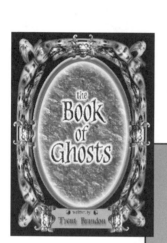